Hungry Devils

And other tales from Vanuatu.

To Dny
Thanks for
Coming!

Bryan W Webb

ISBN: 0615566626
ISBN 13: 9780615566627

Library of Congress Control Number: 2011943399
Natora Press, Neosho, Missouri

Table of Contents

Preface

Vanuatu, the setting of this book, has been our home away from home for the last ten years. Situated one thousand miles east of Australia, Vanuatu is comprised of sixty-five major islands and innumerable smaller isles. Sitting on the Pacific Ring of Fire, Vanuatu is home to numerous active volcanoes and is shaken by earthquakes on a daily basis. The ecology of Vanuatu is surprisingly diverse, from arid windswept ash plains to dense tropical rainforests. The climate of Vanuatu is decidedly tropical with three unbearably hot months, three very pleasant months, and six bearable months.

The people of Vanuatu are diverse. Successive waves of immigration created islands within islands as each succeeding group of immigrants colonized the coastal regions and pushed the previous inhabitants higher into the mountainous interiors. Insistent tribal warfare and the practice of cannibalism colluded to isolate the various tribal groups. This history has produced islands organized like layered cakes, with language and tribal identity varying by altitude. There are more than 120 languages spoken in Vanuatu. The island of Espiritu Santo alone has over 100 of those languages represented and may well be the most linguistically diverse place on earth.

The ethnic diversity extends beyond languages. The native people of Vanuatu, or Ni-Vanuatu are Melanesian; they are typically dark skinned with deep brown eyes and thick black hair arranged in tight, small curls.

Their facial features tend to be delicate and fine boned. Most are short and slim and because of an active lifestyle very strong.

There are, however, significant exceptions. For example, Ni-Vanuatu from the island of Ambae often have long flowing hair that falls in loose curls, the inhabitants of Paama tend to be large and muscular, and the people from the island of Ra are often very fair skinned and their children sport blond afros. Among Ni-Vanuatu, albinism is very common.

Politically, Vanuatu is a parliamentary republic. Members of parliament choose the president, prime minister, and members of the cabinet from among their membership. Because there are many political parties, political alliances shift quite frequently, resulting in a very fluid balance of power. Few prime ministers serve for long. There are three municipalities in Vanuatu—Lanakel to the south, Luganville to the north, and Port Vila, the national capital in the central area. Vanuatu is generally a quiet, respectful, and nonviolent society. The national government in fact exercises only nominal control in the rural areas, where 86 percent of Ni-Vanuatu reside[1] local chiefs mediate most disputes and dispense much of the justice.

The economy of Vanuatu is primarily subsistence agriculture with Ni-Vanuatu meeting the bulk of their needs, from food to shelter, from what they grow in their gardens. The three primary drivers of the cash economy are foreign aid, cattle, and copra (the dried meat of coconuts). Many Ni-Vanuatu engage in the cash economy sporadically, and then only to meet a specific financial need or goal.

Diet varies greatly depending on location. Inhabitants of coastal villages have rich and varied diets with fish from the sea and abundant fruit. Children in the mountain villages nearby often sport the distended bellies typical of a diet nearly devoid of protein and vital nutrients. The lack of protein at higher elevations means that the villagers eagerly incorporate nearly every possible source into their diets from snails to bats. The national food beloved to all Ni-Vanuatu is *laplap*—a dense starchy pudding wrapped in leaves and baked over hot stones.

Melanesian culture is distinctly paternal with the men dominating every area of life. Women are subjugated; many rituals are forbidden for women to even view, they are expected to stoop when walking in the presence of

---

1 CENSUS OF POPULATION AND HOUSING 2009 RELEASE
(Vanuatu National Statistics Office, Ministry of Finance and Economic Management, 31 August 2010)

men in a show of humility, and they must always bathe downstream of the men. Wives are purchased with a combination of cash and traditional gifts. In urban areas, the traditional bride price is often a cultural patina over a romantic relationship forged by the couple.

In rural areas, arranged marriages are far more common, with the couple often not meeting until shortly before the ceremony. Domestic abuse is common and often viewed as a necessary "discipline" for the wives in an effort to maintain good order in the home. A growing women's rights movement is confronting this and many other inequities.

Christianity first came to Vanuatu on November 5, 1858, when John Paton, a Presbyterian missionary, landed at Port Resolution on the island of Tanna. Now, 95 percent of Ni-Vanuatu would label themselves as Christian[2]. The largest denomination is Presbyterian, accounting for nearly a third of all Ni-Vanuatu. Together, the Anglican and Catholic churches comprise another third. The Assemblies of God is the fifth largest church, with 5 percent of the population attending their churches.

While the majority clearly identify themselves as Christian, in fact a strong syncretism has evolved in which most Ni-Vanuatu follow a nominal form of Christianity combined with traditional religions—the spiritual equivalent of covering all your bases. Only 4 percent of the total population exclusively follows the traditional religious customs; this group primarily lives on the islands of Espiritu Santo, Pentecost, and Tanna.

I trust that this brief introduction has helped you visualize this wonderful place. My hope is that through these stories you will get a glimpse of the nation and people that we love and respect so much.

---

2 CENSUS OF POPULATION AND HOUSING 2009 RELEASE
(Vanuatu National Statistics Office, Ministry of Finance and Economic Management, 31 August 2010)

Vanuatu

Vanuatu is the land that I love, my surrogate home, the land of my calling.

Vanuatu is misty mountains cloaked with lush tropical rainforests dotted with quaint thatch villages next to cold bubbling springs.

Vanuatu is cascading waterfalls leaping into picturesque alpine valleys that host dancing rivers which spill onto sugar white beaches before emptying into cobalt blue bays.

Vanuatu is the roaring surf churned frothy white on the teeth of coral reefs and windswept ash plains beneath intimidating volcanoes.

Vanuatu is high broken mountains towering over low coral atolls, luxury high-rise condos sitting opposite rust-eaten tin shanties, hand-carved canoes gliding beneath the shadow of million-dollar yachts.

Vanuatu is crimson sunsets that ignite pebble beaches and make white sands glow pink, coastlines lined with a silver thread of moonlight.

Vanuatu is bright eyes, warm smiles, and open hearts.

Vanuatu is the crash of waves, the rumble of volcanoes, the rattle of earthquakes.

Vanuatu is the toll of church bells, the sound of choirs, women's chatter and children's laughter.

Vanuatu is tribal drums beating in the night, the eerie echo of conch shell horns across high mountain valleys, the roar of tropical downpours smashing onto the dense rainforest canopy.

Vanuatu is an old man in a suit and tie laboring over a pulpit in the tropical heat calling men to follow an eternal God.

Vanuatu is young men in penis sheathes springing from elevated towers with vines tied around their ankles, attempting to appease an ancient god with a symbolic sacrifice.

Vanuatu is glittering black volcanic ash, massive spreading banyan trees, brilliantly colored grass skirts swaying the forest reverberating with ancient chants, a ring of dancers springing into the air, coiling their legs and collectively slamming wide bare feet into the *nasara,* or dancing ground. The ground trembling, crashing rain falls like a blanket across the valley, cutting off the outside world, the rest of the island, the rest of the valley, until time has stopped and all there is is here and now. This is Vanuatu.

Vanuatu is an unnumbered myriad of islands, 120 distinct languages, swarthy swaggering six-foot men from Paama, wiry pigmies from Espiritu Santo, blond children with violet eyes on the island of Ra.

Vanuatu is a Christian nation with a living memory of cannibalism. Its coastal communities have served Christ for two centuries while mountain tribes still sit in darkness.

Vanuatu is proud pagan chiefs, subjugated women, malnourished children.

Vanuatu is pre-Christian villagers blinded by the god of this world, enslaved by sin, fearful of unseen spirits, captive to the twin tyrants of ignorance and illiteracy.

Vanuatu is an unlimited opportunity. In the midst of this crushing darkness, if we go, if we preach, some will hear, some will believe, some will call on his name and be saved. We can change eternity with our actions.

Holy Ground

The mud beneath my feet is oozing black and flecked with bits of brown stone. I am standing beneath an enormous bougainvillea bush; its lower branches have been consistently pruned so that it forms a spreading canopy about seven feet above the ground. Grey wisps of cloud seep through the tangle of branches that form this shelter, leaving behind a heavy dew that falls in large cold drops down the collar of my shirt. This is the community of Ponmuili.

Ponmuili is a group of outlying houses from the village of Lonlipli; it sits high on a narrow ridge dividing two valleys on south-central Pentecost Island. It is the site of a two-day clinic with doctors and dentists from Health Care Ministries. Its primary advantage over other prospective sites is that it lies along the only road bisecting the island. We are here because the villages of the Sa people in this area of Pentecost are *kustom*: they have thus far rejected the gospel. They have no churches. Our hope is that as the villagers see the love of Christ displayed, they will want to come to know him.

Before me is a small, low-slung thatch house. Its newly constructed thatch roof and bamboo walls are still fresh and green, waiting to age to a mellow honey color over time. Its dark interior has a mud floor and is divided by curtains into a number of exam rooms. Here doctors and nurses will treat numerous diseases, stitch up victims of domestic abuse, and pass out loads of worming medicine.

Curious villagers are beginning to gather around us. I don't know if they're drawn by the promise of free medical care or if they're just inquisitive about the white folks. Topless women and girls wearing heavy grass skirts gather in shy, giggly clusters, hiding behind one another but watching everything with bright wide eyes. Little boys with palm fronds wrapped around their penises run and jump in the mud, generally enjoying the excitement of foreign visitors to their village. The men proudly wearing only their *numbas* (a bit of woven mat wrapped around the penis) squat in the mud on wide, thick-soled feet. A few of the men smoke cigarettes of dark homegrown tobacco. Their eyes stare without inhibition at the pale, fully clothed visitors while they share witty observations in the Sa language.

At the door of the clinic, Kathleen Ewing, the team leader, is setting up a makeshift pharmacy. Suitcases full of various medicines and assorted supplies are opened to form temporary shelves. A crude table of rough-hewn boards is set up as her working area. A half wall of bamboo serves to keep the crowd at a manageable distance and prevent pilfering. With her curly white hair and gentle smile, she projects a patient grandmotherly image that suggests she would love to spoil you rotten. In truth, Kathleen, a neonatal intensive care nurse from the States, is a no-nonsense leader with years of experience in leading medical teams on short trips to the Pacific islands.

We—missionary families, two dentists, a doctor, a physician's assistant, and four nurses—gather around the pharmacy, trying to escape the constant dripping. Kathleen gives last minute instructions to the team and answers questions. She assigns exam rooms and charges nurses with the responsibility of either triage or dressing, and I pair the medical personnel with various missionaries who serve as translators and introduce our two native Sa translators. The full mission team is fluent in Bislama, the national language, but we expect to see some patients that speak only Sa.

Kathleen asks me to open the clinic with prayer. After my prayer, she leads the team in song. "We are standing on holy ground, and I know that there are angels all around…." I glance at the clinic building with its dark, dirty interior and look down at the mud encasing my feet, noticing the flecks of brown stone glistening in the all-pervasive moisture. *This is holy ground?* I ask myself.

Traditionally, much of the ground in Vanuatu is considered holy. Ni-Vanuatu deem active volcanoes especially holy, and they hold extinct craters in reverence. One such crater on Tanna is named Itapu, literally meaning "this is the holy place," and a valley there is called Enmantange, or "holy ground." For major construction projects, a cultural survey is required before site preparation can begin. Tabu sites, or holy places, must be marked and preserved.

Christians have holy places as well—Calvary, Gesthemeni, Bethlehem, and Mount Sinai. Ground made sacred by God meeting with man. Individuals often view the site of their own salvation with special reverence. But this, this muddy village in the middle of a forgotten island?

Ground is holy where God meets with man. This muddy house may not be Mount Sinai; however, by the Holy Spirit, God gathered this team of medical professionals here. He led Steve and Kara Jeager as they performed the initial survey. He guided our decision to determine the clinic site. He brought us here together from across the United States, led us to the far side of the globe for one purpose—to meet with the Sa people.

Tears run down my cheeks as I realize that here on this muddy mountainside, God is using us to reveal him. This is holy ground!

Note: Before the outreach was finished, more than five hundred patients had been treated, and over half that number met with God for the first time.

The Price of a Pig

I am sitting on two enormous bamboo logs that have been fashioned into a bench of sorts under the shade of a small mango tree. A steady drizzle fills the air, but I am reasonably dry under the canopy. On my lap, I am balancing a plate of Tanna soup, everything that is available thrown into a pot and cooked until tender. Today the soup includes a small pig. With both hands I hold a pork rib and gnaw the meat while attempting to avoid the hairy skin. This is the first meat I have had all week.

The chief catches me in this inconvenient position. I can't stand because of the bowl of soup, I can't shake hands because mine are full of pork ribs, and I can't talk as I have a mouth full of chewy meat. So I do the classic Ni-Vanuatu greeting—I grunt and wiggle my eyebrows. Sort of a nonverbal, "Nice to see you. How are you?" The chief smiles. "Are you enjoying the pig?" he asks. He waits for me to wiggle my eyebrows in the affirmative before continuing. "You see the lady standing by the table? She brought you this pig. In exchange for the pig, she wants you to tell her the truth about God."

Standing at the end of the table is a short plump lady with a shy smile on her face. I would guess that she is in her early fifties. Here in the bush of Tanna, for a woman to approach a man, especially an important guest such as a missionary, is very difficult. Here the men surround me, and I see the women only as they hurry back and forth from the kitchen with pots of food or dishes, always stooped in an exaggerated show of submission and

7

respect and carefully avoiding any eye contact. But by giving a pig, she has obligated me to talk with her.

I am in south Tanna for a pastor's retreat. This church is one of only two Assembly of God churches in its language group. This language group has over seventy villages, a population of over nine thousand, and only seven churches of any kind, which have a total of less than four hundred members. Most of the villages surrounding us are *kustom*, meaning that they follow the traditional animistic Ni-Vanuatu religions. Even in the villages with a church, only a fraction of the population will ever attend. A priority for me is seeing new churches planted in this area.

I nod my head toward the lady, and she approaches timidly. She sits beside me with her eyes fixed on the ground and speaks in such a low voice that I have difficulty hearing her words.

"Missionary," she says, "I need to know the truth." She tells me she is illiterate, making it impossible for her to read the Bible and discover the truth for herself.

She says that she sent one of her boys to the Catholic school and another to the Assembly of God school.

"Why would you do that?" I ask.

"I thought to myself," she says, "that at least one of them will find the road to life." She tells me of visiting priests, teenage Mormon missionaries, and Baha'i teachers that have passed her way, all telling a different version of truth.

"But yesterday, when you spoke, I felt something I had never felt before, so I brought you a pig so that I could ask you to tell me the truth about God."

How sad to have lived a life in the fog of illiteracy. How tragic that the gospels she had received had been conflicting doctrines that further obscured the truth. How desperate the search for truth that would have you commit your children to conflicting views of God in hopes that at least one would be saved. I began with creation and slowly wove the story of God's plan of redemption. I had no way of knowing what she knew or didn't know about God so I assumed nothing and covered everything.

She nods as I tell the story, gradually becoming less timid and more open, even stealing the occasional glance at my face and daring to make eye contact. We talk for over an hour, with me explaining the scriptures. When I ask if she wants to pray and accept Christ as her savior, she says yes, and there under the mango, I lead her in a sinner's prayer. When we finish, her face beams with joy. She found what she came for; she thanks me profusely and repeatedly.

I think back to the day I found Christ as my savior. I too was illiterate. I too knew next to nothing of God. I understood only that I was a sinner, that Christ was a savior, and that if I asked him to, he would take my sins away. That evening at the altar, Christ did just that in fact, he did more—he gave me new life. Over time, I grew and learned to read. I received constant teaching and was able to verify in the Bible what I had been taught. However, my new friend would most likely never have that privilege.

The tragedy of illiteracy strikes me hard as we finish our talk. I wonder how much of our conversation she will retain. I wonder if someone with a smooth tongue will come by at a later date peddling yet another gospel. I wonder how much of God's plan she will ever truly understand.

"Hold to this," I tell her. "Hold to this and never let go—it is through faith in Jesus Christ alone that we have peace with God." With these words, I give her the essence of the gospel. I had to; that was the price of the pig.

At Least You Are Only Going Downhill!

I am sure that there are worse positions to be in, but at the moment, I really can't imagine one. My legs are sore and trembling, my feet are perched precariously on two slim logs over an open pit latrine, and my stomach, angry over contaminated water, growls and rumbles enough to drown out the sound of the nearby Yasur volcano that is in full-on eruption. My bare hindquarters are a picnic to dozens of malaria-bearing mosquitoes, and I am clutching a handful of leaves since I forgot to bring toilet paper. Oh, the joys of being a missionary! To add insult to my indignity, the small outhouse I am perched in has no door, and a friendly pastor is running off curious youngsters for whom this spectacle is a source of unbridled amusement.

How did I come to be in this position? The path that led me here started at Eniu and ended at Kaugenomaiken. The problem, however, is that the path led through Lauwanpakel. Once I got to Lauwanpakel, then it was a simple matter of four hours of travel by boat and truck to reach Kaugenomaiken. As I started out from Eniu at dusk, Pastor Seni asked in a surprised voice, "You are going now?" Ah yes, there is nothing like being the only one that doesn't have a clue what the path ahead is like.

"Sure," I answered. "We need to get to Lauwanpakel in time to have church tonight."

"Did you bring a flashlight?" she asked.

"No," I answered tentatively.

"Did you bring a backpack?" she asked.

I hesitated. "No, just a normal suitcase. Why? They tell me it is close by."

It took her a minute to answer. "Oh, yes, well, at least you are only going downhill!" That was when I knew I was in trouble.

In Vanuatu, there are numerous expressions that make an experienced missionary quake with fear. They include such comments as, "We are almost there," "There is only one hill," "Really, we have arrived already," and "It is just a small hill," but none strikes fear so deep in the heart as those dreaded words, *"Bae yumi go doan nomo,"* or in English, "It's all downhill from here." Having spent nearly seven years in Vanuatu, I know that these idioms mean the exact opposite of what the words would imply.

Thankfully, Pastor Samuel volunteered to carry my suitcase, and as a man totally without pride, I had no difficulty surrendering it to him. Besides, I had my hands full with gifts from the previous villages. I marveled that after seven years of treks through the boonies of Vanuatu, I had allowed myself to be so unprepared and naively believed the pastor when he told me it was a short walk. I had no backpack, no flashlight, and no toilet paper. I was wearing khakis and sandals with holes in the soles. What did I have? Three coconuts, two chickens, a bag with my Bible in it, and slung over my back, my fishing pole. I was ready for anything!

At first, the path really did go downhill through the middle of a swamp filled with wild sugar cane, and I wondered if maybe everything was going to be okay after all. Then the sugar cane ended, and I had a clear view of what lay ahead—not one, not two, but three peaks rose before me. Each one added to the last to form an imposing wall between me and the coast, and on the coast was Lauwanpakel. These were the kind of peaks that made you gasp, "There is no way!"

Twenty feet ahead of me was Pastor Joni Lava, at least ten years older, nine inches shorter, and fifty pounds heavier than me. I watched him as he began the laborious climb before us and vowed that I would not let someone older and heavier outclimb me. Under no circumstances would I ask for a break or a drink or even pause on the path unless Pastor Joni did first. It is a vow I came to regret; my, but that fat man can climb.

When we reached the top of the final peak, we paused to rest under the full moon. Behind me lay the dark interior of Tanna. On the right side, the sky glowed a dull red from the fires of Yasur, Vanuatu's most famous volcano. Before me, the moon laid out a silver path across the ocean. About five miles down the mountain to the south was the glimmer of light from the church at Lauwanpakel. "See," Pastor Joni told me. "Really, we have arrived already."

Gethsemane

"I'm sorry, Pastor. Your son has appendicitis; however, our surgeon is gone. He should be back in three or four days. It may burst before then…"

Not the words you want to hear while sitting in the emergency room of the Northern District Hospital in Santo, Vanuatu.

The walls may have been painted a dingy yellow. It was hard to tell through the layers of grime and the sections where the paint was peeling off in thick petals. As I contemplated the nurse's words, a rat ran down a cord hanging at my son's bedside.

It was dark outside. The hot tropical air sat heavy and still, thick with the foul odor of vomit, urine, and feces, ripe in the day's heat. Not your typical hospital smell. This was nauseating. The stillness of the night air was broken by moans and occasional sharp cries of pain. Numerous languages bounced off the walls of the courtyard, some soft and resigned, others strident, urgent, demanding.

A mother ran from a nearby room into the emergency room, her hair unkempt, her clothes filthy from days of sleeping on the floor of the hospital, her face distraught. "My daughter, my daughter! Something is terribly wrong! Oh, please! Can you get a doctor?" But there was no doctor. There was no help. I listened to her daughter's cries of pain grow faint until they were replaced by the wails of grieving relatives. I bowed my head in prayer. "Oh, God, we need your help."

Early that morning, Bryan, our twelve-year-old son, had awoken with what appeared to be a routine childhood stomach bug. However, by late evening he began to complain of severe pain on his lower right side.

With tears in his eyes, he asked, "Daddy, am I going to die?"

"Of course not," I answered. But now I was worried.

I have never regretted being a missionary, but this was a trying night. I prayed, "Oh, God, you have got to help my boy." My mind went to Erokor Island, where the gospel first gained a foothold in Vanuatu. I remembered the little mission church and the graveyard beside it, filled with the small graves of the missionaries' children.

The Father paid an awful price to declare his love to this world, and ever since, missionaries have laid down their lives and the lives of their families following his example. This may have been my Gethsemane, but I did not want this cup. With tears in my eyes, I whispered, "God, I will trust you, no matter what." It was a very long night.

Early the next morning I received a call from AIG Assist, a service provided to Assembly of God missionaries. "Mr. Webb, a private jet is en route from Sydney, Australia. It will have a medical team on board that will include a surgical consultant. They'll be bringing all the equipment they need. They will assess Bryan and, if possible, transport him to Sydney." A few hours later, Bryan and I were whisked away by jet. After a four-hour flight, we were met at the airport by an ambulance.

At Sydney Children's Hospital, a smiling nurse with a musical Australian accent greeted us. "Hello, I think we are expecting you!"

There couldn't have been a greater contrast between the two emergency rooms. Sydney Children's Hospital was celebrating children's day. We went through gossamer veils into a magical kingdom. The room was brightly lit and air–conditioned, its walls colorful and cheerfully decorated. Branches and flowers hung from the ceiling. The nurses and doctors were dressed in cheery costumes. A play therapist circulates around the room, playing games, blowing bubbles, spreading cheer everywhere she went. A doctor examined Bryan immediately and then sat down at a workstation with several other doctors just five feet away. Imagine that: Doctors! In the hospital!

Less than an hour after our arrival in Sydney, Bryan and I were taken into the operating room. The surgeon told me frankly that he was not optimistic. Thirty-six hours after the onset of the sickness, Bryan's skin had taken on a sickly pallor, and the surgeon anticipated that the appendix had burst.

The doctor allowed me to stay with Bryan and hold his hand as he drifted off to sleep under anesthesia. Then a nurse led me to a waiting room. I bowed my head and asked my Father to watch over my little boy, so thankful that he had so far. The surgeon came in with the news forty-five minutes later. It was a big, fat, swollen appendix, but it had not burst. Bryan was fine.

I have to tell you, I have never been more thankful to be an Assembly of God missionary than I was at that moment.

Santo

"Stop here, Missionary," Pastor Dick told me. I slowly brought the truck to a halt at the crest of the hill. To my left an open pasture dotted with orange trees gently sloped up to meet a thickly forested hillside. On my right a cluster of orange trees, their branches loaded with bright yellow orbs, obscured the view. I stepped out of the truck, happy to stretch my legs after a two-hour drive over the bumpiest roads I had ever driven. As a new missionary, I was on my way to Big Bay for the first time.

Pastor Dick led me through the cluster of orange trees to a rocky out-cropping. The ground fell away before me, and I was treated to a panoramic view of the entire northern part of Santo. Before me, still and quiet as a sleeping baby, Big Bay lay cradled between the arms of Santo.

Two massive peninsulas jut out of the north side of the island. The one to the east is covered with low hills and extends thirteen miles from the body of the island. The one on the west is over thirty-seven miles long and consists of high rugged mountains. Its mountains are black with distance, and wisps of low-lying clouds lay tangled on their peaks. Those dark mountains pull at me. They seem to embody the phrase, "regions beyond."

In 1606, the explorer Pedro Fernández de Quirós, sailing under the Spanish flag, became the first European to see Santo when he landed on the shore of the bay. He christened the island La Tierra Austrialia del Espíritu Santo, or the Southland of the Holy Spirit. He then named a nearby river the Jordan River and embarked on establishing a settlement called New

Jerusalem. The cannibalistic bent of the locals soon led him to abandon his efforts. The only lasting heritage of his visit is the modern name of the island—Espiritu Santo, or Holy Spirit, Island.

Espiritu Santo is a big beautiful island. It is seventy-two miles long and thirty-seven miles wide and lusciously green. It is ringed with some of the world's most scenic beaches, coral gardens, and azure seas. The interior is crumpled into a collection of jagged mountains. These tear at the soft underbellies of clouds that vainly attempt to skim by unscathed.

Their ruptures in turn produce daily deluges that give birth to thousands of streams and waterfalls. Plateaus along the east and south coasts are planted with orderly rows of tall coconut palms. The wide open land under these palms provides grazing land for tens of thousands of cattle. These copra and beef farms provide the basis for the island's economy.

Scattered over the island are wrecks and ruins from World War II. Abandoned Quonset huts, the shells of warplanes, ammunition dumps, thousands of glass Coke bottles, and unused artillery shells litter the island. Offshore lay the wrecks of the USS *Calvin Coolidge* and USS *Tucker*.

During the war, the United States maintained a presence of one hundred thousand troops here with a seaplane base and two airfields. Famous units such as the Black Sheep Squadron based here. James Michener wrote *Tales of the South Pacific* on a hillside overlooking the nearby islands of Aesi and Mavia.

The forty thousand islanders that call Santo home are a diverse group. They speak more than one hundred different tribal languages. Many could be considered merely dialects of each other, but the locals have assured me that others are as different as English is to Japanese. The south and east coasts are the most densely populated, the interior and west coast only sparsely settled. The tribes are as different as their environments on the island. On the east coast, tall strapping men run cattle plantations or glean their living from the sea, while high in the misty mountains of the interior, compact muscular pygmies leap from stone to stone over river rapids spearing fish or freshwater prawns and garner all they need from the dense cloud forests.

Research Espiritu Santo and you will find that nearly every source affirms that the locals are "mostly Christian." Why would missionaries give their lives in such a place? There are two primary reasons. First, although most Ni-Vanuatu consider themselves Christians, they do so often in name only. For many, being a Christian means little more than joining a particular political party or community club.

The second reason is what compels me to continue to invest in Santo: the thousands of villagers who live in an area from Big Bay down through the interior to South Santo that stretches nearly all the way to the west coast. The majority of villages in this area are kustom villages; there are no churches, no schools, and no Christians. I'm driven by the thousands of villagers living without a gospel witness, who are illiterate and unable to discover the truth for themselves. That an island named after the Holy Spirit should be home to such darkness offends me.

A significant portion of our work in Vanuatu is on Espiritu Santo. Hope Clinic in Big Bay reaches into these unreached areas with compassion. Jubilee Christian School is a part of educating a new generation and giving them the skills needed to know God. Sanma Bible Training Center endeavors to train pastors to serve in these rugged, unreached areas, alleviating the crippling need for pastors. Sanma Adult Literacy School will help to pull back the veil of darkness that has held these tribes captive for far too long.

When I think of Santo, I see those dark mountains that frame Big Bay, and to those waiting in the darkness, my soul whispers, "A great light is coming!"

Angels in the Dark

Friday night is always a noisy place in Chapi, the village where we live. Numerous kava bars, a liquor store, and a nightclub ensure that our village doesn't get much rest on the weekends. Since the sun has just gone down, the partying is just getting started, so I decide it is safe for a walk to the village store. Little do I know...

So much is familiar as I make my way down the village road. The inky black that follows a tropical sunset swallows up any pale light attempting to escape from a kerosene lamp or brave bare florescent bulb. The warm moist air scented by the smoke of cooking fires flows over your skin like water. The noises—a pig grunts beside my foot in chorus with the retching that follows each shell of kava the men drink—how could you ever forget those noises?

So much is the same, yet since we returned to Vanuatu, following our furlough. We have been confronted with many changes—few of them good—such as the growth of nightclubs, an increase in alcoholism, the introduction of marijuana, and a steep rise in theft and violent crime. We lived here in this village for four years and never had one thing stolen. Now in less than two weeks, we have had thieves steal the clothes off the line in our yard, chairs off the porch, and Bryan's bike.

As I walk, I mourn the changes and pray for revival. It seems to me that even the level of friendliness has changed. Before when strangers passed in the darkness, they exchanged respectful, quiet greetings. Tonight several of my greetings have been met with stony silence. Is my voice too quiet? Are they ignoring me? For a second I pause before an especially dark portion of the path. I can see the glow of cigarette embers along the sides of the road. Is it safe to pass this way?

I chide myself for my squeamishness and continue. I pass the red glowing points of light and smell the odor of homegrown tobacco. I pass barking dogs, sure I can feel their breath on my legs.

On the way home, things are better. The dogs are lying peacefully beside the road, and the people I meet in the darkness respond to my greetings and even engage in cheerful conversation. As I turn the last corner in the road, a young man running full speed in the darkness nearly collides with me. *What has he done?* I wonder. *Is he a thief that has just stolen another pair of my pants? That little devil!*

Then I see them. Some twenty men are milling restlessly in front of the gate to my home. "Father, help me, watch over my family," I pray. Who are these men? What do they want? Are they waiting for me?

When I reach the group, I notice that one of them is lying on the ground, moaning in pain. He, too, is praying. "Father, forgive me. Father, forgive me." A neighbor approaches me with a sheepish grin.

"What's going on here?" I ask.

He shrugs. "He was swearing loudly and breaking bottles."

"And?" I ask.

"Some boys beat him. Now he is being quiet."

I go inside to find my wife, Renee, shaken. She tells me a drunk man was swearing loudly, making threats, and breaking bottles at our gate. She says how afraid she was and how she was wishing I was home when she heard a rush of noise followed by quiet. I wonder, did I meet a devil or an angel in the dark?

Wok Boe Blong Jisas

Pastor Dick Joel Peter is one of my closest friends and my cultural mentor in Vanuatu. My first contact with Pastor Dick was over the telephone. Renee and I were new missionaries. Having just recently arrived in country, we were still in the daze of jet lag. We were staying in a dank, musty apartment under the mission house at Joy Bible Institute in Port Vila. Numerous visitors had come to welcome us to our new country of service, but their names and faces had morphed into an indistinguishable blur. I used the phone in the mission office to call him. I felt I should introduce myself since I would be working directly with him once I arrived in Santo. His enthusiastic voice cut through the haze and set him apart as a singular person. "Missionary, we are so glad you have come to Vanuatu! We have been waiting for you here on Santo!"

The warmth and sincerity in his voice caused me to trust him immediately, and I shared my two most pressing concerns with him—housing and transportation. "Don't worry, Missionary," he told me, "I will find you a truck and a house." True to his word, within hours he had found us an excellent truck at a deep discount. Within a week he had lined up a half a dozen prospective homes for me to view, one of which would be our home for the next seven years; it, too, was deeply discounted. These two early experiences revealed a key aspect of Pastor Dick—he is a fixer. Give him your problems, and he loves to use his connections and influence to make things happen.

When I asked the missionary who had preceded us on Santo if he had any advice, he gave me one suggestion—have coffee once a week with Pastor Dick. One month after we arrived in Vanuatu, we moved to our new home in Santo. Even before we had furnishings in the house, Pastor Dick and I began a tradition that would carry us through many storms. On Monday mornings, we would meet at the Natangora Cafe. He would buy a newspaper, introduce me to at least ten or fifteen new friends as they came through the coffee shop, and over a cup of coffee and a muffin, he would tell me stories to teach me the values I needed to master in order to understand Ni-Vanuatu culture.

Pastor Dick was one of the early Ni-Vanuatu converts of Ron Killingbeck, a missionary to the French territory of New Caledonia. As a young man, Pastor Dick was a hopeless alcoholic; he was hospitalized with a burned-out liver and waiting to die. Missionary Killingbeck came into the room and prayed with him. That day God healed and saved him, and he joined the small band of Ni-Vanuatu migrant workers who were being discipled by the missionary. Soon after they decided that he and a handful of other young men would be sent to the Bible school in Fiji.

After graduation he was summoned to Santo by Killingbeck, who had moved to Vanuatu and was planting a church in the town of Luganville on Santo. As a young single man, Dick was placed in charge of the new church and given responsibility for promoting the Assemblies of God in a vast spread of islands then known as the Northern District. In the twenty-five years that had passed before I met him, the church had grown to close to four hundred members, he had planted an average of a church a year in the outlying islands, and he had served the Assemblies of God fellowship as district superintendent, deputy general superintendent, and general superintendent. When we arrived in Vanuatu, he held the offices of district superintendent and deputy general superintendent.

I was and am honored that a man with so many responsibilities and a great ministry background was willing to spend so much time with me, a rookie missionary, to teach me the ropes. Pastor Dick didn't just give of himself ministerially, he also opened his home and his heart to our family. He has displayed such warmth and caring toward our children that we often refer to him as their *Bubu*, or Ni-Vanuatu grandfather. I came to realize over the years that he views training missionaries and exercising pastoral care for them as a part of his ministry.

Understanding Pastor Dick even when you know the language he is speaking is a challenge. He speaks English with a thick accent and at a rapid-fire pace that sounds like the staccato of a machine gun. He loves to tell jokes; he starts off with a chuckle to let you know that he thinks what is coming is immensely funny and then takes off like a race car with his heavily accented words banging off of one another in a verbal demolition derby. You sit opposite, leaning forward and trying to distinguish a few words, trying to ascertain the general flow of thought when his flow dissolves into gut-wrenching laughter. Many of those early Monday mornings, I found myself laughing just because he was; his mirth was contagious even though I had no idea what the joke had been.

A few short weeks after we meet, he decided to force me out of my comfort zone and proceeded to speak only Bislama to me. I sat through those first few Bislama coffee sessions immensely frustrated. Slowly, my comprehension increased, and I discovered to my delight that his Bislama was significantly easier to understand than his English. In hindsight, I am so thankful that he didn't create a comfortable English bubble for me to inhabit but instead forced me to master my adoptive language.

Fast forward ten years. I was standing on the floor of what would be the Sanma Bible Training Center chapel. There was lots of work to be done, but I was out of money and volunteers were scarce. Pastor Dick, pastor of a large church, district superintendent, father in the faith to thousands, was there beside me. He was dressed in grubby work clothes, he held his well-worn knife in his hand, and sweat streamed down his face. He worked and talked without missing a beat, lamenting the fact that the young pastors and today's youth were unwilling to be here with us.

He paused for a moment and leaned on his knife. Tears began to stream down his face. "You know, Missionary, all those years ago, I started out my ministry by cutting the grass on the Bible school campus. I said, 'God, if you will let me work for you, it won't matter what the work is; I will be your work boy.' Now all these years later, here I am. It doesn't matter what others will or will not do. I will always be a work boy for Jesus!"

In Mark 10:44 Jesus said, "Whoever would be great among you must be your servant." (NIV) I cannot think of a higher title than "Wok boe blong Jisas."

The Pastor and His Wife

I am sitting on a wooden bench in a small smoke-stained thatch house. The walls are split bamboo that have been woven into a diamond pattern. The roof is a thick thatch of natangora leaves. Rough wooden benches line the walls, and a crude wooden table made of unfinished planks occupies one corner. The dirt floor is covered with mats woven from the leaves of the pandanus plant. The thatch is a mahogany brown, but everything else, the walls, benches, table, and mats, are a light honey color.

I am sitting with my elbows on my knees and my eyes on the floor mats, the only culturally acceptable position for a meeting of the kind we are having now. I am joined by a pastor and his wife. The pastor has several days' growth of beard, and his eyes are red from crying. Across the room from him sits his wife of over twenty years. Her hair is uncombed, her dress is dirty, and her face is puffy. She leans heavily to one side, obviously in pain. Their eyes, too, are locked on the floor mats.

I don't even begin to know where to start this conversation. The tension and pain in the room are palpable. A week earlier, the pastor had attacked his wife in a fit of rage. He had beaten her cruelly, knocking her to the ground, kicking her until she no longer moved, and then he had choked her. By the pastor's own confession, only the arrival of her sons kept her from dying. Now a week later, she is finally able to get out of bed.

Members of American churches often believe that their overseas counterparts are more spiritual or holy than they. I am not sure where this idea came from; maybe missionaries coming home on furlough were disappointed by their home churches' decline in spiritual fervor or materialistic bent and perpetuated this legend by holding up their converts as unrealistic examples. Maybe the simple, unmaterialistic lives of poorer Christians convict and inspire American Christians, who are wealthy in comparison.

More than one visiting pastor has lamented that he wished his church was as dedicated as the saints in Vanuatu. "I wish my people were half as hungry for God's Word as these folks are," a frustrated American pastor told me. I had to bite my tongue. One fellow who considered himself a very discerning soul told me, "God has his hand on that young man right there; he will do great things," as he pointed to a serial adulterer who frequently beat his wife and stole from his employer.

Forgive me if I am breaking a cherished illusion. People are the same everywhere. We are all sinners; that is, we have committed sin, and by our nature, we are prone to continue to do so. Paul said in Romans 7:18, "For I know that in me [that is, in my flesh] dwelleth no good thing." (KJV) That nature is crucified when we come to Christ. We bury it in baptism but it is not eradicated. We rise and walk in new life, but the battle remains—will we walk after our sinful nature or after the Spirit?

If you have been a Christian long, you know that we all want to live in the Spirit but far too often find ourselves slipping back into patterns of behavior that are certainly not Spirit led. Continue to engage in the "innocent" wants of the sinful nature, and you will be shocked to find yourself doing things that repulse even you.

Sitting across from me, the pastor weeps as he confesses his sins and offers me his resignation, not just from his position in the church but of his credentials. He is committed to continue to follow Christ, but as a church member and not a leader. His wife also weeps as she recalls the details of the attack; she chokes out what have to be bitter words: "I forgive him."

In times like these, the gap between Vanuatu and America seems enormous. "What would happen to me if I were in America?" the pastor asks. "You would go to prison," I tell him, all too aware that far too often the perpetrators of domestic abuse in America go free with few or no consequences for their actions.

In Vanuatu, the woman is the possession of the husband. He pays her father for her, and she becomes his property. Culturally, wife beating is of little consequence. Even in this case, the local chief said, "I tried to get the pastor to not say anything to you. If he had kept quiet, we could have just covered this up. There is no need for him to step down as pastor."

Missionaries are often attacked for destroying culture, yet the truth is that by teaching God's Word, we are confronting some false concepts in every culture. Each person does have equal dignity before God regardless of sex or age, physical or mental stature; this is true in every place.

As a missionary. I have counseled those who have cheated on their spouses, men who have beaten their wives, fathers who have abused their children, and even child rapists. In my heart, I rage against them and their actions. I want to punish them. I have watched in frustration as the justice system fails to hold them accountable. Yet as much as I hate their sins, I know this: "But God commendeth his love toward us, in that, while we were yet sinners, Christ died for us." Romans 5:8 (KJV)

The claims of Christ are valid, not just in carpeted cathedrals. They also must be true in this honey-colored hut. Christ did not die for us because we were worthy. Forgiveness is not just for nice people. Healing is not just for bodies, but also for hearts, spirits, and marriages.

We close our counseling with prayer, but there is no miracle. The bruises still remain, not just on the pastor's wife's body, but also on her heart. The gulf between them is wide and will take months to heal. What they have started is a journey—of forgiveness, healing, and hope possible only in Christ.

Breast-Feeding Brides

On the ground in front of me was a captivating sight: an enormous pile of taro, a traditional root crop, pandanas mats, and half a cow, all topped with a number of live roosters. Women from the island of Ambrym rent the rain-heavy air with wails as they mourned the loss of a daughter. I could feel the tense, expectant breath of the crowd pressing around me. There were well-dressed relatives from town, villagers in tattered clothes, and men and women wearing only a few leaves or a single piece of cloth, and some wearing bones through their noses.

I was watching the purchase of a bride in the Ni-Vanuatu tradition. A young woman, completely covered in white powder, was led into the middle of this crowd. She was brought before the man who would be her father-in-law. After a short speech, money changed hands, about six hundred dollars. Then the mother-in-law led the bride away by a rope, like a cow or horse that had just been purchased. The imagery was gripping.

I had been invited to this ceremony by Chief Norman of White Grass to celebrate his and a number of other weddings. This was a series of firsts for me—the first time I had heard a wedding sermon with a strong admonition against polygamy, the first time I had heard the pastor passionately proclaim in a wedding that beating your wife is not acceptable, the first time I had seen seven couples wed in one ceremony, and the first time I had watched a bride breast-feed her infant while saying her vows.

Is the presence of newborns in a wedding ceremony an indictment against the church? Does it indicate a shortage of morality in the body of Christ? Far from it! This is what happens when the church penetrates areas that have long sat in spiritual darkness. You see, each of those couples getting married were already a family. Most were from a tribal group known as Mal Mal, bushmen of the middle of Santo, bluntly called pagans by many in Vanuatu. They and their kinfolk have been some of the most gospel-resistant people in Vanuatu. They solemnized their marriages because of the effect of the gospel on their lives.

Instead of being a condemnation of the church, the fact that nursing mothers were a part of this ceremony was cause for celebration. It vividly illustrated that the gospel elicited not merely an emotional or intellectual response, but also the kind of transformation that alters every part of life and culture. That for the first time these families saw the need to solemnize their commitments to one another and to commit to monogamous relationships signaled the triumph of the gospel.

Only the year before, one of the participants had told me he was holding off on marriage until he could decide how many wives he wanted. Only the month before, I had had the privilege of leading another participant to come to know Christ. Only the week before, a third participant came to me saying that after he was married, he planned to go to Bible school and prepare for ministry to his own people.

I do not know when I have ever seen a more beautiful wedding.

They Bought Tanna for the Gospel with Their Blood

Honestly, climbing has never bothered me too much. Besides that pounding sensation in my chest, my tongue hanging out, and the spots before my eyes right before I get to the top, it has never been a problem. Going down is another matter. After just a couple of miles, my knees ache, my thighs throb, and my calves turn to trembling mounds of Jell-O. I can see only a few feet before me in the moonlight. To my right is the face of the mountain, but to the left I see the ocean. The path is narrow and twisting, the ocean is a long way down, and I have no way of knowing if I am climbing down the side of a gentle slope or a stark cliff face. It is going to be a long night.

Five hours after we started, we have covered about eight miles, gotten lost in the dark at least three times, and arrived at a barbwire fence. "We're here," Pastor Joni announces. I see no church, no school, no houses, and no lights. This he announces is the last water before the village and the best place to bathe. Everyone else is enthusiastic about swimming in the river, and I tag along. Really, what choice do I have?

We make our way down a vine-covered embankment to a dry creek bed. Scattered along its length I see stretches of stagnant, scum-covered water. Numerous cattle tracks lead into each pool, and suspicious clumps float in the scum. A pungent barnyard odor assaults my nostrils. As a missionary, I try to always have a can-do attitude, but I draw the line here. "Guys, I think I'm going to take a pass on this bathing spot." Pastor Joni looks up with surprise; he has already stripped off most of his clothes, and with towel and soap in hand, he is obviously looking forward to a refreshing dip.

The moonlight reveals a look of perplexity on Pastor Joni's face. "But, Missionary, this is it. They will only have rainwater to drink at the house. We always bathe here."

"Well," I reply, "I guess that I'm just going to be a smelly missionary." My guides and companions are stunned. A smelly missionary? This just cannot be! But since the missionary refuses to cooperate, they reluctantly make their way to the church at Lauwanpakel.

Upon arrival, I am standing on the site of a London Missionary Society's mission in Tanna. Before me is a scene of beauty and peace. The smell and taste of salt spray fills the air. Silver moonlight plays over the ocean in synch with the rhythm of the waves as they swell and break over stone reefs. The rough stone bluff I am standing on sits at the back of a narrow passage to the sea. At the mouth of this passage, ocean swells find the only gap in the reef. Here, these swells, tired from the journey of their lives, shoulder their way between the two rocky reefs that define this passage. To the left and right, lesser waves break, reduced to churning foam, yet in the middle a pregnant engorgement forms as a too-large swell forces its way through a too-small opening. Once past this laborious passage, the tension passes, and the swell reclines in the comfort of the narrow inlet like a tired old man slowly laying his aching limbs on his bed, and ends its journey with a soft sigh on the pebble beach twenty feet below me.

Tonight the view is serene and peaceful, but I wonder what foreboding tales this inlet told to those who came before me. I envision a three-masted schooner riding the swells beyond the passage in the reef. Coming toward me in the moonlight is a longboat, its strong oars pulled in a steady rhythm by sturdy strong seamen. They are attuned to the night, marking the cadence of the waves, carefully timing their passage through the reef. But their nervous eyes watch more than the reef, for before them lies the island of Tanna, filled with dark, untamed mountains; mist-filled craggy valleys; a fuming, lava-belching Mount Yasur; and pagans who are eaters of men.

Among the seamen is a young woman. Ridiculously out of place in her heavy European clothing, she sits with a refined dignity in the middle of the longboat. The moon casts a beam on her face and, delighted with the whiteness it finds there, shines with extra vigor to better illuminate this most unusual visitor. On the pebble beach, surrounded by luggage trunks and inquisitive locals, stands her young husband; he strains to read the emotions at play on her face. Is there an eagerness, an enthusiasm for the challenge ahead? Or do the eyes hold dread and a fear of the unknown? Perhaps just a steady determination to meet whatever lies ahead with dignity and grace. I cannot tell. Maybe her young husband, who knows her better than I, can read the mysteries of her face, but for me tonight, the vision is too dim to know with certainty.

Together they step into a new land to do exploits for God. Over the next few years, they will create what is known as the mission compound: the residence for the missionary, homes for those friendly locals that make their lives possible, a well for water, gardens for food, a church, a school, and a simple clinic. The goal of the compound is to draw Ni-Vanuatu to them, lead them to Christ, and teach them to read his words.

In time, such ideas will fall out of favor; today missionaries and church leaders speak with scorn of the idea of mission compounds. Rather than create a compound to draw in locals, the missionary must go to the locals, learn their customs and languages. It is called the incarnational model. I have no quarrel with such ideas, but for that first young couple, the compound would serve as a cocoon for the gospel in Tanna; a small beachhead of light in a land of overwhelming darkness. It served to wrap the missionaries and those first curious locals in a semisafe cocoon where growth and an amazing transformation could take place. For them to leave the compound meant almost certain death at the hands of cannibals.

In the end, not even the cocoon could spare them. When that cocoon broke, what had been was dead, but what emerged over the next one hundred years is an island transformed. Is there still darkness? Yes, entire valleys remain unreached. But look at what has changed—cannibalism is a distant memory, young wives are no longer strangled after their husbands' deaths, tribal warfare has ceased, and missionaries sharing the gospel can travel safely from coast to coast.

The paramount chief of North Tanna insisted that I be treated as a chief or dignitary on my recent trip. When I protested saying that I was just an ordinary man coming to work beside him and his people as a brother, the chief rebuked me. "To us, a missionary is no ordinary man," he told me. "You see, they bought Tanna for the Gospel with their blood."

Scattered Seeds

The bushman read the jungle floor for me. "Here, Missionary, this was a huge redwood," he said, pointing to a blackened, rotting stump. "And this is where they milled it," he told me, pointing to a slash of new growth in the jungle. "See this? This is where the workers sat down to rest," he said. "Look, you can see they ate an orange here; they scattered the seeds and now orange trees are growing." He pointed to some orange saplings. A sad, almost pensive tone entered his voice. "They came this way and threw out these seeds never knowing a tree would grow here. One day there will be oranges here, but they will never eat them."

Eight years previously I had arrived in Santo. I was eager to learn about my new home, so I gathered together a few local pastors, and we went exploring in my brand-new Toyota pickup truck. For an hour we bumped along the east coast highway. It seemed that each turn and each bridge had its own story. I was introduced to the world-renowned Champagne Beach and shown the place where a previous missionary had rolled his truck. Just past Champaign Beach but before the village of Hog Harbor, Pastor Dick recognized a friend. "Pull over, Missionary; I want to talk to him."

His friend was an elder for the local Presbyterian church. My memory of him from that day is of a wide shiny face cut by deep wrinkles staring at us in shock from under the shade of a floppy broad-brimmed hat. You have to understand that being greeted by Pastor Dick is a bit like a verbal assault. He has a thick accent, and he speaks fast and loud in a culture where slow, soft communication is the norm. Once recognition set in, the elder's expression changed from shock to pleasant surprise, and an expansive smile revealed multiple gaps in his teeth. After a few minutes of pleasantries, we were on our way. "He is a good man," Pastor Dick told me. "One day we will convince him to leave the Presbyterian church and join us. Whenever I see him, I always ask him if he is ready to become one of my elders."

Over the next eight years, I would often meet this gentleman in town. I would gently kid him about changing churches. We would exchange laughs and each go on our way. It became a bit of a standing joke between us, Pastor Dick urging him to discover the Full Gospel, and he adamantly defending the Presbyterian church. I never dreamed he would ask me to his home to preach.

A few months ago, we welcomed a new missionary couple to Vanuatu, and I was asked to preach at the welcoming service. I took my text from 3rd John, verses 7 and 8 of the NIV: "It was for the sake of the Name that they went out, receiving no help from the pagans. We ought therefore to show hospitality to such men so that we may work together for the truth." I stressed three points—that the missionaries had come for Christ's sake, that missions is about partnership and that far from home, family, and all that was familiar, these new missionaries desperately needed the family of Christ to embrace and befriend them. I urged the believers present to invite them into their homes and get to know them.

That night a young man named Thomson met me after service. "Missionary, while you were speaking, God touched my heart. I couldn't stop crying. I want you and your family to come to my home for a meal." Over the next few weeks, he and I developed a friendship. One day he bought me lunch. On another occasion we met for prayer together. On yet another he worked with me for a day at the Sanma Bible Training Center. Each time we met, he reaffirmed his invitation: "My mother and father want you to come; they are going to fix laplap for you."

It seemed that every time we planned to go as a family to Thomson's village, something would come up that interfered with our plans—a medical emergency forced me to go to Australia for surgery, a crisis in a local church demanded my attention. He asked us to come the first Sunday in July, and I agreed without checking the date, only to find it clashed with Renee's plans to host the American community at our house for a Fourth of

July celebration. "Okay, Missionary, I understand, but next week you have to come," he told me when I let him know of the scheduling conflict.

Today was finally the day, and an hour out of town down that same road I had followed eight years ago, just before the village of Hog Harbor, bright pink gateposts adorned with wine bottles welcomed us. As we turned into the dirt drive between the posts, a small village became apparent. There was an odd mix of houses; bamboo huts with thatch roofs, wooden shacks with walls of timber of varying lengths topped by rusting roofing iron, and a cement block building with its dull gray walls unpainted. Four cows munch contentedly on the open lawns. Citrus trees abound; oranges, tangerines, grapefruit, and enormous pamplimus hang heavy on their branches, and overripe fruits litter the ground. To our left was a pole barn, its rafters strung with balloons. A table heaped high with fruit sat at the entrance, benches were lined up neatly across the floor, and a table and pulpit stood at the far end. We were expected.

As we pulled in close to the pole barn under the shade of an orange tree, Thomson, followed by his father, came to greet us. His father was Pastor Dick's Presbyterian friend. He greeted us with that same wide smile and urged us to eat some fruit before the service began. "Today, Missionary, you have come to scatter some seed. We will have to wait to see what the fruit of it will be."

One sows...

One More Hill on a Sea of Islands

Dusk is falling, and I am standing at the top of a deep red clay bluff in North Tanna. Mile after mile of lesser hills and valleys spread out before me painted a deep emerald green by the thick tropical foliage. Here and there a garden or village clearing exposes the red clay, like scrapes on the skin of this green landscape. The swiftly fading sun makes the exposed clay fluoresce a burnt orange. The wind that dries the perspiration on my face carries the woodsmoke smell of hundreds of cooking fires and hints of the coolness of the night to come.

Seni Irongen, the pastor of Full Gospel in Eniu, stands beside me. This pastor is at least six feet tall and has broad shoulders and a face that shows no fear. She is also, to my knowledge, the first woman pastor in the history of Vanuatu. "They're out there, Missionary, village after village of kustom people from here almost all the way to the coast." She has touched the quick of my heart, as such people are the primary reason I am in Vanuatu.

A letter from Seni's husband, Tom, is what brought me to Tanna. In it he asked for a missionary for North Tanna: "Would you please send a missionary to North Tanna? We need a school and at least an aid post for medical care." He went on to explain that he and his family had donated four acres of prime property and even cleared it in anticipation of a missionary coming.

After receiving Tom's letter, Gary Ellison, president of Joy Bible Institute and I decided that the only proper response was to go see. Because of Gary's tight schedule at Joy Bible Institute, the task of going to see fell to me. So I set out on a survey of the island of Tanna to determine validity of the needs Tom described.

On my survey trip, I visited all twenty-one churches, numerous outstations, proposed sites for mission homes, the Tafea Bible Training Center, and the future Tafea District Headquarters. I traveled through unreached valleys and met with members of the Jon Frum cargo cult, some current and others who had come to the Lord and become members of our churches. I met with most of the senior pastors from Tanna, the executive committee for Tafea District, American Baptist missionaries, and numerous chiefs, including the paramount chief for North Tanna.

My conclusion? A missionary could:

- Invest his or her life in the Tafea Bible Training Center and help raise up a rich source of leaders for Tafea and beyond.
- Develop a plan for ministry to the Jon Frum cargo cult.
- Do pioneer evangelism among truly unreached villages and the nominal Christians in the south.
- Start Christian schools in villages where there are none.
- Provide medical aid in many places that lack even the most basic care.

One chief cried as he told me the story of woman after woman that had died in childbirth because they had no clinic for miles. A missionary who devoted his or her life to Tanna would be one of the most loved missionaries ever.

Tom and his family have picked out this bluff for the missionaries' house. The scenery is incredible, the breeze is refreshing, and the site is clean and ready for building. If only it were that easy. If only all I had to do was ring up headquarters in the States and say, "Send me one more missionary." In reality, all I can do is tell my leadership, "If another missionary should become available..." I patiently explain to them that every country in the world is crying for missionaries, and the best thing they can do is pray to the Lord of the Harvest that he will send more laborers into his fields. Would you join me in prayer? Who knows, maybe you are that laborer that the Lord will send.

My Health

I am standing in front of a group of thirty pastors and church leaders. We've come together for a time of spiritual retreat, prayer, and study of God's word for the next twenty-one days. The evening prayer time is concluding, and most thoughts have turned to food. Mine, however, have turned to a little more personal problem—my health.

Most missionary stories are about success, great victory over impossible difficulties. Missionaries are often portrayed as spiritual heroes striding from conquest to conquest. Some new missionary recruits have felt betrayed when they realized that those blazing fires of victory are really brief bursts of light in the midst of the mundane.

This story is not about victory. It is about frustration.

Over the last twelve years of service on the mission field, a frustrating pattern has evolved. When I've planned ministry trips to hike through unreached territory to share the gospel from village to village, preach a pastor's seminar, or build a building for a new church plant, I develop a nagging infection.

The timing of these infections is hugely suspicious. They have forced me to cancel or abandon countless ministry trips. In fact, I never develop them while in the United States or when engaged in ministry that keeps me at home. They only develop when I am engaged in the ministry God has called me to out there in those forgotten places.

The first day I notice a burning sensation when voiding; then next day I feel like I am passing razor blades. The women reading this will understand this better than the men, since my affliction is far more common in among women. The same anatomical fluke that allows me to develop the infections in my urinary tract in the first place allows it to race through my system. Untreated, I move from slight discomfort to life-threatening kidney infections in the space of a week.

Visits to the doctor's office have become depressingly predictable. The doctor reads over the results of my tests with a worried frown. "This is highly unusual," he tells me. "Men don't develop these infections." "How nice for you," I think. One doctor even went so far as to tell me that although one out of three hundred men share my anatomical fluke, only 5 percent of those ever develop infections. Great. Well, I may not be one in a million, but I am something like one in thirty thousand. Lucky me!

As the doctor sits, his tone changes to one of confidence. "But now that we know the problem, we can fix it." I wish I could share his confidence. By this time, I have seen numerous specialists, had six surgical procedures, and taken just about every antibiotic known to man. Many doctors have promised a cure, but none have delivered. I have learned the best I can hope for is a reprieve.

More frustrating than the sickness is the fear. For twelve years I've asked myself every morning, *Am I okay this morning? Has the infection come back today?* It is a haunting, nagging, restless fear, like an unhealed wound to stand in the midst of the jungle hundreds of miles from any medical care and question, *Has the infection returned?* Yet, I feel I know the cure—give up, quit, throw in the towel, pack my bags, and scurry back to the safety of home, abandoning those who are sitting in darkness.

Maybe I would still develop infections if I did quit, but at least I would be in a country with adequate medical care. To visit the doctor wouldn't involve a two-day trip that costs over three hundred dollars in airfare alone, only to have him tell me, "I really don't have the equipment here to properly test you."

At this point, believing God *can* heal me is simple, but believing God *will* heal me is hard. My father asked me, "Has God ever promised to heal you?" I guarded my words as I answered. *Promised me?* I thought. No, God never gave me a personal promise to heal me. In fact, when I approach heaven for healing, it seems I hear the door slam in advance of my arrival, and when I draw near, I hear the double bolt being drawn.

But today, standing here in front of these pastors, I determine in my heart that faith will triumph over fear. I confess my fear to the pastors and ask them to pray with me for two things: freedom from fear—that if God never heals me, I will never live another day of my life in fear—and for healing; that for as long as I live, I will never have another one of these infections. Pastors gather around me in prayer; surely God will answer.

Today the infection is back. I can't say I understand. Did I not believe? Maybe; I am willing to accept the blame. Is this my thorn in the flesh? A messenger sent from Satan to buffet me? Maybe; I don't know. I can't claim to have great revelation like Paul.

This one thing I know: "Though God slay me yet will I trust him." I will, with every strength that he gives me, fulfill the calling he has placed on my life.

Philippians 1:20 says, "I eagerly expect and hope that I will in no way be ashamed, but will have sufficient courage so that now as always Christ will be exalted in my body, whether by life or by death" (NIV).

A Heavy Basket

A deep fissure split the hills to my right; vines clothed the gash with thick green cloak. To my left the ocean, tortured and harassed by the constant wind, took its frustration out on the rugged broken coastline. Before me a braided rope of gurgling streams tied the two together. Car-sized boulders lay scattered along the streambed like marbles thrown by a giant. The streams danced over and around them, here joining hands, here springing apart, swirling into deep pools carpeted green by velvety moss, frothing with foam under small waterfalls, and gleefully splashing the proud boulders that tried to hold themselves aloof above the frolicking water.

Standing along the banks of the stream and perched on various boulders was a crowd of more than a hundred men, women, and children. A group of pastors worked at enlarging and deepening one of the pools, patiently removing moss covered-stones from the bottom and replacing them at its base to raise the level of the natural dam. Today was baptism day.

When I reached the streambed, I removed my shoes and slowly picked my way across the pebbles and stones that made up its bed. Laughing bare-footed children skipped past me, oblivious to the course gravel causing my feet so much grief. Clear, cold water surged up to my waist as I stepped into the newly renovated baptismal pool. I raised my voice to give some last-minute instruction about baptism before motioning for the first candidate.

An elderly gentleman made his way toward me. Two young pastors helped him across the broken streambed. He wore a lavalava, the traditional wrap of a Tanna kustom chief. The skin on his legs, hands, and face was mottled with age. This man, Samnouiaken, was one of the highest ranking kustom chiefs on Tanna and a significant leader both in the local system of government and in the traditional animistic religion. He was old enough to have served with American troops during World War II. My heart swelled with emotion as I thanked God for giving me the opportunity to lead him to Christ and baptize him before it was too late.

As I watched him make his way into the baptismal pool, my mind went back to the conversation we had four days before. That Wednesday evening I had preached from Matthew 3 about the need for repentance. He and several other high-ranking chiefs had listened intently yet chosen not to respond to the altar call. After the service, Samnouiaken thanked me for my sermon and praised my Bislama language skills but remained uncommitted.

Thursday morning when I returned to the crusade site for breakfast, he and his fellow chiefs were waiting for me. They greeted me with a chorus of appreciation for the sermon and again commented on my Bislama. I was getting embarrassed by the attention and started to move away when the chief reached out and grasped my arm. He looked up at me through bloodshot and rheumy eyes as he held my arm in his trembling hand. "Missionary, we discussed your sermon until dawn. The thing that troubles me is, what if all these years I have been leading my people down the wrong road?"

That evening I heard a collective gasp from the crowd as, aided by two walking sticks, he responded to the altar call for those who wanted to accept Christ as their savior. Throughout the evening, people expressed their astonishment that he was abandoning the traditional religion he had followed and taught his whole life to come to Christ. "Missionary, I never dreamed I would see him take this step," was echoed repeatedly.

There in that pool the crowd heard his testimony and witnessed his commitment to follow Christ in his life. Tears welled up in my eyes as I laid him back into the pool and watched his head slip beneath the smooth surface of the clear, cool stream. "In the name of the Father and of the Son and of the Holy Spirit."

Later that day, Pastor Japen shared the story of a conversation he had had with the chief on the way down to the stream for the baptism. Pastor Japen said that he noticed the old chief had a clouded expression on his face, as if something was weighing on him.

He asked, "Old fala, is something bothering you?"

"It is just this basket I am carrying," Samnouiaken replied.

Pastor Japen double checked, and sure enough, the chief was carrying nothing other than his walking sticks. "What's in your basket?" he asked.

"All of my kustom knowledge," the chief said.

"Old fala," Pastor Japen replied, "the things in that basket can't save you. Only Jesus can do that."

"I know that," the chief replied. "It is just that it is really heavy, and when I get to the water, I am going to lay it down."

Arrival

Shalom Assembly of God is a small white chapel sitting on a three-acre patch of green grass surrounded by brilliantly white sand. This evening the sun has set behind the mountains to the west. It no longer shines here, but its last rays light up the clouds above in soft red and orange hues. The light from the clouds reflects on the sand, making it glow a soft pink.

Everywhere I look I see beauty—the palm trees in the distance standing dark against a red sky, the sand glowing pink. The pulpit inside the church is surrounded by a dazzling arrangement of flowers; such a wealth of tropical flora would make a New York City florist green with envy. Behind the pulpit, the chief's wife is leading the worship. She is a stately matriarch with silver highlights running almost too perfectly through her hair. Her face is the kind that draws little children to her, the face of a grandmother: confident, yet kind and benevolent.

This is my view. On the opposite side of the church sit our two new missionary associate couples, one of whom arrived only yesterday evening. I wonder what their view is. Twice now in the last three months I have stood at the airport in Santo waiting for a new couple to arrive. As that small twin-engine plane lands and makes its way across the tarmac to our little terminal, I wonder what is going through these young couple's minds.

I found arriving on the mission field to be surprisingly anticlimactic. I was very aware of a call of God on my life concerning missions from the age of eleven. I made my way into adulthood anticipating that it would be my life's work. I spent the necessary four years in Bible school, always with the intention to prepare for missions. Dorm room discussions, classroom debates, and prayer band meetings all revolved around this future.

Between classes and around the chapel altar, I daydreamed of when I would take my first step onto the field. I imagined myself clear eyed and confident, striding off the plane onto the soil of my host country, somewhat of a Neil Armstrong moment, "One small step for man" You get the idea. Surely I would lead someone to Christ before leaving the airport. I was sure that it would be a moment of overwhelming emotion as my life's dream would begin to be fulfilled.

The reality is that getting to the mission field is hard work. It is preceded by twelve long months of endless travel from church to church and from meeting to meeting with pastor after pastor. Any last vestiges of pride are stripped away by making endless appeals for money to perfect strangers. You must gather and fill out mountains of papers to gain a visa from your new "home."

If that were not enough, there are then a series of exhausting medical tests to anticipate any medical needs you might have once you are so far from home. After your blood has been drawn, your urine tested, your lungs x-rayed, and your privacy invaded by other unmentionable tests, you are sent to the dentist for a rather ominous X-ray of your teeth to be placed on file for identification.

Once the funds are in, the visa secured, and the doctor satisfied, you begin to say good-bye. You sell or give away everything that will not fit in a few suitcases. I remember sitting on the floor of our living room surrounded by suitcases, two preschoolers, and a few scattered papers, too emotionally exhausted to close the last suitcase and pack the bags in the van.

In a week that passes in a blur, you visit grandparents, aunts, uncles, cousins, and friends.

Each visit is precious, tearful, and filled with promises rarely fulfilled and an additional drain on what emotional reserves you still have intact. At the airport, bags are searched, tickets are lost, tempers flare, tickets are found, and apologies are made while teary-eyed grannies and grandpas or papas and nanas cling to dazed and confused little ones.

For two days you comfort your preschoolers on the plane and drag them through strange airports, eat airplane food, relieve yourself at twenty thousand feet, sleep in an impossibly narrow chair, and dream of a shower.

You arrive on the mission field having not showered or shaved, wearing clothes you have slept in for two days, and in a state of complete and total emotional, physical, and dare I say it, even spiritual fatigue.

Many have compared the transition from one culture to the next with the experience of losing a loved one, not an altogether inaccurate comparison. In time you adjust. Your sleep cycle synchronizes with the sun, you learn where to buy groceries and how to speak the language. The constant sharp pain of homesickness subsides to an occasional dull throb, and you come to know, accept, and then love the place, culture, and people God has sent you to. You see the beauty in the sunset once again.

After a few years, the field becomes home. Local foods are pleasant, and you even miss them when you are away. Local people are your surrogate family, your friends and confidants. Local scenery warms the heart. The local language flows like a smooth stream from the tongue and becomes almost indiscernible from English to the ear. It gets easy to forget what it felt and looked like when you first arrived.

I know what I see now, but can these new arrivals see the beauty in the sunset?

Mari Kor

I am sitting under a mango tree in Pastor Simon's front yard trying to ignore the mosquitoes biting my ankles, silently praying that none of them are carrying malaria. The single florescent bulb hanging in the church thirty feet behind me is all that breaks the darkness. The light illuminates half the faces of friends, leaving the other half in shadow. The conversation is low and respectful, the kind you would hear in a waiting room of an intensive care unit in a hospital. We wait with Pastor Simon. Mari, his wife, lies dying in their bed not twenty feet from us. The quiet hum of our conversation is punctuated by the sounds of saws and hammers coming from the church. They are building a coffin for Mari.

I don't remember the first time I met Mari. After I had come to know her as Pastor Simon's wife, it was years before I knew her name. One of the oddities of Vanuatu is how difficult it is to know who is married to whom. Because of strict prohibitions on any displays of public affection, husbands and wives avoid each other in church functions. Once you have determined who is with whom, you are still a long way from knowing a wife's name. Women are rarely introduced by name but instead referred to as the mother of their oldest child or, more commonly, as the woman that belongs to that man. That was how I knew Mari: she was the woman that belonged to Pastor Simon.

Mari was a large, round woman with a quick smile and a ready laugh. Unlike most Ni-Vanuatu women, she was not shy. She would look you straight in the face with a twinkle in her eye. She loved to tease. She fearlessly chided the menfolk, including the missionary, when they didn't meet her approval. She wore huge, brightly colored Mother Hubbard dresses that were cut far too low at the neck, and I am quite sure that she is the first woman I have ever known to have a hairy chest.

Thanks to my close relationship with Pastor Simon, I slowly began to get to know Mari. She was a first-class pastor's wife. She loved God, her husband, and her family. She loved the church and labored endlessly in it. She rallied the women and led them in ministry. She corralled the children and made them join her in the front row of church. She was the center of her church and family.

Her chief complaint with me was that I took her husband away from home too much. Pastor Simon is a great preacher and teacher and thus a great traveling companion for a missionary. When we would return home from a crusade, church planting trip, or preaching tour, Mari would be waiting beside the road for her husband's return.

She would give it to me from both barrels. "Missionary, we need the pastor here."

I gave her the nickname "the complaining woman." I would turn to Pastor Simon and ask,

"Are you sure you want to stay here with the complaining woman?"

Mari's diatribe would dissolve into laughter. "Missionary, you are bad," she would tell me.

Last Christmas, Renee and I bought a bed for Simon and Mari. That night was the first time in twenty years of marriage that they had not slept on the floor. I never would have dreamed that before a year was out, it would be her deathbed.

It started with a fall; Mari was a robust woman, so any fall is serious. Because she had severe back pain Simon took her to the local hospital for X-rays, and before the day was over, Mari was paralyzed from the waist down. She would never regain the use of her legs.

Over the next few months, she visited the hospital for various infections, each one a little more serious than the last. The last week, the paralysis began to spread. Soon Mari could no longer speak and could move only her left arm and her eyebrows.

I sat with Pastor Simon in the hospital room as she repeatedly raised her left hand high in the air. Her daughter played twenty questions with her to try to understand what she might need. Finally, Pastor Simon asked, "Are you worshiping God?" With her eyebrows, Mari answered yes. That was the last communication Mari would ever make. Later that day she slipped into a coma, and her family brought her home to die.

Our subdued conversation is interrupted by an urgent whisper. "Papa, come." Pastor Simon leaves us and hurries into their simple two-room home. A few seconds later, heartbreaking cries rend the night air. Mari is gone.

In Vanuatu the death of a loved one is mourned in stages, with the final period ending at one hundred days after the death. This Christmas, we gathered to mark the one hundredth day for Mari. As we wept, Mari celebrated the advent of our Lord in person.

Immanuel

"There is only one small hill." With these words of assurance ringing in my ears, I followed Samson, the first graduate of Sanma Bible Training Center, up to his home village to open a new church where Samson would be the pastor. I had my first doubts about the size of that hill after climbing three hours and learning we were only halfway up. After more than five hours of climbing, we topped out at more than four thousand feet. One small hill indeed!

In these misty heights, I discovered a whole new Vanuatu. While the inhabitants of the coastal plains grew all manner of fruits and vegetables, residents of these hills grew only taro and island cabbage. Most of Vanuatu prides itself as being a Christian nation, but these tribes boast that they follow Satan. Most people in Vanuatu are modest to the extreme; these proud chiefs forbid the entrance of those wearing clothes into their villages. In place of churches are temples dedicated to the local gods; instead of hymns, kustom dances fill the air. While other Ni-Vanuatu strive to walk in the Spirit, these men dance on coals of burning fire.

Our destination was Maluicalua, whose villagers were eager for the church to come to them. This was the first place I had ever gone to plant a church where the people completed the church building before I arrived. We had arrived for a week of services with student pastors from Joy Bible Institute ministering. The response was overwhelming. I even had the privilege of naming the church, Immanuel, and conducting the first wedding ever performed in this village. I watched as a man wearing only a loincloth used a stone as a hammer to hang the church sign.

The final night was a moving service. Pastor Simon Kor, our presbyter, ministered but an air of sadness permeated the service. The people were concerned. One said, "You have come, you have let us taste the sweetness of the gospel, but now you are leaving us alone. We do not know how to worship God. We do not know how to read, so we cannot read the Bible. What will we do when you are gone?"

Pastor Simon smiled and reminded them that Samson would be returning to serve as their pastor. Then he said, "Do you know the meaning of the name of your church? It means, '*God i stap witem yumi*' [God with us]." A realization filled the room. Faces lifted. Spontaneously, the people broke into applause. The missionary was leaving, the presbyter was leaving, the students are leaving, but God was staying with them!

These simple tribal people's response to this truth, two thousand years old, but so new to them, moved me to tears. How often you and I have celebrated Christmas, enjoyed the feast and festivities, basked in the warmth of the love of friends and family, yet yawned our way through a pastor's best efforts to remind us of the miracle of Immanuel, God with us.

This Christmas, enjoy all the festivities to the fullest. Drink hot chocolate, play in the snow, go see the Christmas lights. Enjoy your family. Believe me, we would love to be with ours. Savor the sweets and all the good food. But most of all, join with the villagers of Maluicalua in celebrating this wonderful truth, *God i stap witem yumi*!

Restoration

One thing about islands: you can't escape.

The islands of the South Pacific are small. Some are mere postage stamps. I have spent weeks on islands on which you could stand on the beach on the east side and throw a stone into the water on the west side. The highest point on one island was six feet above sea level; at king tide, the occasional wave would roll over the entire island.

Island communities are small, too. Santo's population of forty thousand is spread out in villages that average less than fifty people. Only a quarter of a million people inhabit the entire nation of Vanuatu, and as far as Pacific island nations are concerned, Vanuatu is a giant. Take almost any two Ni-Vanuatu, give them enough time to compare family histories, and they will soon find a connection. In a place where a second cousin is considered your brother, extended family circles overlap like ripples on a pond to create a nation of family.

In times of trouble, tension, or conflict, Americans often want to move on with their lives, put the past behind them, get out of Dodge, or make a fresh start. Outlaws were warned to be out of town by sunset in the Old West with no regard to where they might go. In a nation where millions of people regularly leave the area where they are from, putting your past behind you and starting over really is an option.

When conflicts are small, we don't relocate. Instead, we change banks, phone companies, grocery stores, or restaurants. Rather than practice conflict resolution, we practice conflict avoidance. "I just can't deal with those people," we say. It is easier to just move on.

The ease of escaping the past has infected our church culture as well. Many in church leadership no longer practice any form of official discipline. To do so is deemed futile; the disciplined member merely relocates to another community of believers in the same town. A competitive, numbers-driven approach to church growth allows this unhealthy practice to continue. In cases as benign as a conflict with the church board or as tragic as a moral failure, moving on is often considered the only, if not the best, option. This has led to a crisis in the Catholic Church, as abusive priests were relocated rather than expelled by church leaders. In a new environment, the abusive priest who leaders should have removed from ministry, could trade on the reputation of those who had preceded him rather than be known for his own soiled past.

In my fellowship, pastors who fall into moral failure and repent are removed from the ministry for two years and placed in a rehabilitation program. After two years, their credentials may be restored, but even then, they almost always serve in a new town, away from the scandal of their past. In a new town and a new church, sometimes a restored pastor is able to truly leave the past behind them.

Life is different on the islands, where locals have only one grocery store, two hardware stores, and two phone companies to choose from. The customer is not always right, and complaints are met with a "so what" attitude. You have to deal with those people whether you want to or not. The point is that avoiding conflict doesn't work for very long. There are no other options. But it goes deeper than that—there are no secrets; you cannot hide from your past.

Being forced to live and interact with people you would rather avoid obliges you to recall a forgotten Christian grace—forgiveness.

Last year I watched the life of a pastor fall apart. In a fit of rage, he beat his wife of over twenty years nearly to death; by his confession, only the intervention of his sons saved her life. Two weeks later his youngest son was arrested for possession of drugs, and two weeks after that, his wife left him. I was there the day he surrendered his credentials. "Missionary, what would my discipline be in America?" he asked me. "In America, you would be in jail for attempted murder," I told him. "We wouldn't be discussing discipline. You would be finished in the ministry."

Things are different on the islands. He faced no legal repercussions for beating his wife, the charges against his son were dismissed, and his wife returned after six months. The presbyter gave him six months' discipline and asked me to minister to the pastor, his family, and his church. I argued forcefully that he disqualified himself from ministry on several counts.

"Besides," I said, "where could he ever go to escape the stain of his past? Everyone knows what he has done."

"Go?" the presbyter asked me. "Why would he go anywhere?"

I sat in stunned silence as his words sank in. For the rest of his life this pastor would never escape what he had done. He would stand in the pulpit as a sinner redeemed by the grace of God, and everyone would know it. No pretending.

The presbyter was asking for a lot more than a pastor to live with his mistakes. He was asking a battered wife to forgive her husband, a betrayed son to forgive his father, a father to forgive his son, and a church to forgive their pastor. Not to merely mouth the words, but to live them daily, indefinitely.

Those six months were a journey of redemption and reconciliation. Many tears were shed. Many regrets were expressed. Last Sunday I watched as the pastor and his wife stood facing the presbyter before the entire community and were restored to their ministry. My mind still questions the fitness of this pastor for ministry, but my heart wonders if the ease of escape we have in America has cheapened this grace called forgiveness.

"Brethren, if a man be overtaken in a fault, ye which are spiritual, restore such an one in the spirit of meekness; considering thyself, lest thou also be tempted" (Gal. 6:1 KJV).

Dietary Hazards of Being a Missionary

I watched as he was carried into the hall as if he were an ancient king. His litter sat on the shoulders of four muscled young men who strained under his weight. Slowly and carefully, they marched to the head table, where he would take his place of honor. The only thing missing was trumpeters to herald his arrival.

Once he came down to eye level, I could examine him more closely. His skin was a rich chestnut brown, what hair remained on his head was midnight black. His face, round and fat, rested on an enormous double chin. The fat squeezed his eyes into a perpetual squint, and his mouth curved into a self-satisfied smile. Once at the table, he remained perfectly still. Closer examination revealed that he was nailed to the litter. He was a pig.

I was in the fellowship hall of Shalom Assembly of God in Nambualou, and we were celebrating the tenth anniversary of the church. After the required speeches by the assembled dignitaries, it was time to eat. I made my way down a table laden with taro, kumala, rice, fish, fowl, and laplap of every possible variety and slowly built up my plate. When I reached the head table, a young man, one of the litter bearers, presented me with a slab of roast pig.

My slab was nearly a foot long, three inches wide, and five inches thick. The leathery skin on top was crusted dark brown and still had a significant remnant of hair. Underneath, on the right side, was a two-inch pearl of gray, moist meat. The rest was the delicacy of a Ni-Vanuatu feast: creamy white, jiggling, glistening fat.

As a missionary, I have been called upon to eat many things outside of normal American cuisine, and I pride myself on my willingness to eat nearly anything to humor my hosts. I experienced the first order of offensive foods—raw fish, pig skin, fish heads, and horse, dog, and cat meat—early on in my missionary career. More exotic foods such as bat, wood-grubs, sea slugs, and fish guts took a bit longer. When I discuss food with Ni-Vanuatu who meet me for the first time, I can see their respect for me rise as we discuss each delicacy, while the Americans look at me like I am crazy.

It is possible to not only acquire a taste for, but to truly enjoy, foods that would make most of my fellow countrymen nauseous. Laplap, the national food of Vanuatu, has to be choked down by most newcomers; however, over time, it is possible to develop into a laplap connoisseur, quite picky about the kind of laplap you eat and the region of the country it comes from.

I will eat a few favorite kinds of laplap till I am sick. Mind you, that is not hard to do since many of the areas I travel through have no plumbing or soap, and the cooks wash their hands only during their weekly bath. The same unwashed hands that change the baby's diaper, wipe the child's nose, and hold other things we don't want to discuss handle my food.

Other foods sound repulsive but in fact are surprisingly delectable. I held out on fish guts for many years. I remember gagging the first time I saw a young man snatching the best bits as he cleaned the fish. However, the sautéed entrails of a fresh-caught yellowfin tuna are not fishy tasting at all and can only be described as delicious. I have huddled around a small fire on the beach with my fellow fishermen and greedily eaten an entire skillet of fried tuna livers by myself. Sharing can be difficult with something this tasty.

The dilemma is what to do when you are presented with foods that you consider downright hazardous to your health. Some villages have such poor hygiene that I plan my visits to avoid meal times. I refuse to eat some kinds of fish; I have seen fellow missionaries less discerning than myself nearly die from fish poisoning. I shudder to think of the effect this slab of pork fat would have on my arteries.

I glanced down at the slab of shimmering fat on my plate; it continued wiggling for a few seconds after I took my seat. I come from a family with a frightening history of heart disease. My mother and brother have both undergone heart bypass surgery. I do my best to watch my weight and exercise. In our own home, we rarely eat anything fried and avoid high-fat foods. But what would I do with this slab of lard I have been served?

Ni-Vanuatu eat meat only on rare occasions—weddings, deaths, holidays, and feasts to honor special guests. They eat protein so rarely that every part of the animal is prized: the head, feet, ears, tail, skin with hair remaining, gristle, and even entrails are consumed with enthusiasm. If the teeth can chew it, the Ni-Vanuatu will eat it. The fat of the animals is the most prized. To be given fat is to be shown great honor. To refuse it would surely be an insult.

When I first became a missionary I tried discreetly tossing such delicacies under the table to the waiting dogs. However, having nearly lost my legs to ferocious dog fights, I since adopted a better strategy. Before I took my seat, I looked around to find the skinniest teenage boy and sat beside him. I noisily made a show of chewing the two-inch pearl of meat off my slab, purposefully smearing my face and hands with grease.

Then when the crowd was distracted, I passed my gnawed pork fat to my new friend.

He inhaled it before anyone noticed the switch.

A Bag Full of Holes

I have a long-standing policy about mountains: I only climb the ones with people on top.

After coming to Vanuatu, I quickly learned that climbing mountains was one of my least favorite things to do. Something about the burning sensation in my legs, seeing spots in front of my eyes, a wildly pounding heart, and gasping for breath while clinging to the near-vertical side of a mountain contradicts my idea of a fun time. When confronted with climbs in Santo's rugged interior, I always ask my guide at least twice, "Are you sure there are people up there?"

It seems impossible that people would choose to live on the top of a mountain, miles from the nearest road. I have no ambition to climb a peak merely to see the world from that vantage point or for bragging rights. I gladly leave such exploits to fools and photographers.

But today, however, I have made an exception. The island of Gaua is one enormous volcano. This huge dome is topped by a massive crater lake, which is home to millions of freshwater shrimp and eels that are larger around than telephone poles. At the rim of the lake, a fantastic waterfall plunges nearly to the sea. At the center is a smoldering cone belching clouds of ash and steam. Minerals from the volcano venting into the lake stain the water myriad colors. Ruins dot the bottom of the lake. If you are willing to swim with the intimidating eels, you can see the remains of stone houses from a prehistoric civilization scattered under the water. It just sounded too good to miss.

Gaua is an easy mountain to climb. While most mountains in Vanuatu require you to crawl on your hands and knees through a mossy tangle of vines or cling to toe- and handholds up cliff faces, Gaua is gentle. In the prehistoric past, Gaua hosted a far more significant population than it does today. They terraced the entire mountain for growing crops, and though the rain forest has overtaken them, the terraces and the stone steps leading from one to the other still remain. Climbing Gaua is more like a walk in a park than climbing a mountain.

At one point during our climb, we come upon the ruins of an ancient stone house. The walls have caved in, undoubtedly a victim of the endless earthquakes that plague volcanoes. However, the stonework that remains is breathtaking. Arches and circular windows were cut into the stone with such precision that you would swear it was the work of modern machines. One such house is completely enclosed in a gigantic banyan tree. A path was cut through the tree, and it takes me nearly a full minute to walk through it.

Once we reach the summit, I know it was well worth the trip. The volcano puts on a spectacular show, spewing ash and steam thousands of feet into the air. The lake and waterfall are everything that was promised and more. Pieces of driftwood pulled from the lake are saturated with the mineral-stained water and have become works of art colored with deep reds and yellows. I can clearly see the shrimp and eels, even from the shore. I am glad I have broken my rule.

On the way down, we follow a different path. Led by a group of teenage guides, we all but run down. We stop, amazed, when we break free from the rain forest and step into a neatly tended kava garden. My guides look around startled. This is their island. They are sure that they know every community and village. Yet here high up on the mountain is a large garden they haven't seen. Where there are gardens, there is a village.

We follow the path of gardens until we see the outlines of a village ahead of us. Our guides, tense and alert now, have lost the carefree spirit that compelled them to race through the jungle earlier. As we approach the village, we see a family wearing tattered clothes standing beside their hut. We wave a welcome and are greeted with a single word, "Mora!" Our guides stand speechless, but I recognize the greeting as being in the language of Paama, an island hundreds of miles south. "Mora," I shout in return. "Tahos?" "Good morning, Is all well?"

Here, high on the mountainside, is a small community of people from Paama. They welcome us into their village, and we hold an impromptu church service. Several villagers make a decision to follow Christ, and they let us know that they would be happy for the pastor of the church in the coastal village to come and hold services with them on a regular basis.

After our service they tell of how they came to Gaua and how they came to live high above all the other villages. Given the size of their kava gardens, I am surprised to see them living in such poverty. Kava takes years to come to maturity but is normally a very lucrative crop.

When I question them on this, they bring me a mud-stained plastic bag. At the bottom are a few coins corroded together. They explain that their chief took a ship to Vila to sell their last crop of kava. When he returned, he wrapped the money in a plastic bag and secretly buried it. Shortly after that, he fell ill and died. The villagers knew they had a stash of cash, but they didn't know where it was. A year later one of the men found the bag; however, by that time water had penetrated it and the huge bundle of paper notes had all rotted away. All that was left were a few corroded coins.

Their story reminds me of Haggai 1:6: "he that earneth wages earneth wages *to put it* into a bag with holes." (KJV)

How much better if they had followed Christ's teaching in Mathew 6:20, to "lay up for yourselves treasures in heaven, where neither moth nor rust doth corrupt, and where thieves do not break through nor steal"? (KJV)

Where are your treasures?

Write Them On the Posts of Your House

I slide the four-wheel-drive stick into low, slipping the gearshift to first and slowly easing off the clutch. I feel the cable tighten, and the truck pauses momentarily as if it were gathering its strength and then begins to inch forward. Behind me, a log, thirteen feet long and a foot wide at its narrowest point, edges out of its resting spot. The local volunteers working with me cheer and race to jump on the truck for the half-mile trip to the building site.

When I visit a church in the Unites States, I am often asked to describe a typical day. "What does a missionary do on a day-to-day basis?" they ask. I can't answer for other missionaries, I can only speak for myself, but there is no such thing as a typical day! One day is reports and newsletters, one day is teaching and preaching, another is hiking through the jungle to reach a remote village, and then there are days like today. Today I am pulling logs out of the bush.

The log behind me is a Java cedar, which looks nothing like the cedars in the United States. Its leaves are round and full, not needle-like, and its bark is smooth, not papery. When you cut its bark, instead of clear sticky sap oozing out, drops of blood well up. The sapwood of the Java cedar is a pale pink, and the heartwood is deep burgundy, almost too intense to be

77

real. This log's bark and sapwood have been removed. The heart of the log is over a foot wide, dense and heavy—a significant piece of timber.

The road I follow is really a tunnel through a solid green mass of tropical rain forest. Enormous white wood and milk trees tower above me, stretching up more than sixty feet before the first branches spread out from the trunk. Yet these trees are hidden, cloaked behind a dense canopy of vines. To reach the already fallen logs, we have carved out a path through the jungle with bush knives and a chainsaw. The vines and undergrowth have been cut just wide and high enough for the truck to pass through, creating a hot, damp, dark, mosquito-infested green tunnel.

These logs are so dense and hard that termites and woodgrubs cannot eat them. After being felled by the winds of a hurricane, they have lain on the floor of the rain forest, some of them for over thirty years. Slowly, the branches, bark, and sapwood rot away, but the heart, or as the locals call it, *natora*, remains. I am pulling them out of the dense bush of the campus of the Sanma Bible Training Center to serve as the posts for the chapel and classroom. Before the day is over, I will have hauled thirteen of these posts out of the jungle.

In the local style of building, the posts are the critical element of construction. The strength and permanence of the structure depends on the type and size of the posts. An insignificant garden house that will be used for only a season uses small posts of common wood that will deteriorate quickly. A *nakamal* or men's house that is expected to serve for a decade or more uses posts of hardwood of a moderate size. However, a building that is to serve generations uses these heavy natora. I have often come upon abandoned villages in the jungle where the only thing remaining is the posts, standing like forgotten sentries. Some of these ancient posts predate the memory of any living Ni-Vanuatu.

A local chief comes by to inspect the thirteen posts that we have towed from the bush. "No, Missionary, these will not work," he tells me. "I thought you wanted to build a building that would last." His tone is almost accusing. "You need true natora."

I am a little frustrated. These posts are natora; they have lain on the jungle floor for years untouched by bugs or rot. What more could he want? He explains to me that these logs, while great above ground, will rot once buried. Only true natora, tropical teak, a wood so dense and heavy that it sinks in water, will stand the test of time.

In Deuteronomy 6:7, Moses tells the children of Israel, concerning the law, ""thou shalt write them upon the posts of thy house." (KJV) While Moses may have envisioned decorative calligraphy adorning the posts of their homes, I tend to doubt that's what he meant. Rather, I think his message was the same as what the chief was trying to tell me: if you want to build a home that will last, you have to use true natora; in our lives and in our homes, that means the Word of God—only it will stand the test of time. Trends and lesser truths will quickly rot away, but the Word of God will abide forever.

However, when it comes to building the campus for Sanma Bible Training Center, teak is also way out of my price range. When I tell the chief that since I am on a limited budget I have to use what is available rather than purchasing teak, he looks frustrated. "Why didn't you ask me? I have plenty of natora."

I try to explain that I know he has plenty but that I am afraid to ask because I could never afford to pay for it. He asks me to come with him in his truck and takes me to a pile of enormous teak logs by his home. "I had my sons cut them and prepare them for you," he said. "All you had to do was ask."

Last week they delivered the first truckload of teak logs to the building site.

Pentecost

Trembling with adrenalin, the young man stood before the naghol tower, which had been built after the pattern of a banyan tree, a maze of strong vertical posts and seemingly haphazardly placed horizontal supports. It soared above the cleared hillside with small diving platforms jutting out of the downhill side. Determined not to feel fear, he fastened his eyes on the highest diving platform, a hundred feet above him, and began to climb.

In the grass clearing before the tower, hundreds of his fellow Sa tribesmen had assembled. Like him, the men were clad only with penis sheaths, the women only in flowing grass skirts. The men beat dried bamboo posts into hardwood sounding boards in an ever-accelerating cadence, slamming their wide bare feet into the ground in a shuffling dance and filling the air with deep, guttural chants. The bare-breasted women leaped in time to the men's rhythm and punctuated the chants with high-pitched shouts and whistles.

High atop the tower, the young man's maternal uncle greeted him. His uncle firmly grasped the young man's wrist and lifted him the last few feet onto the platform. There his uncle tied the split ends of carefully chosen vines around his feet. The other ends of the vines were already attached to the platform, and their length had been carefully measured so that his head would merely brush the ground as they broke his fall. As the young man gazed out over the scene before him, his head spun. Despite all the promises he had made to himself, fear froze his heart in his chest.

He felt his uncle's rough, strong hands lift him to a standing position. Below him, the cadence of the bamboo posts and chants reached a frenzied pace. The women shrieked and whistled. The ground spun beneath him, and he grasped the handholds with all his strength. His uncle had seen this before and knew the shame the young man would face should his courage fail him. With a branch of *naggalat*, a stinging nettle, he whipped his nephew's bare back. The sharp pain of the naggalat cleared the young man's mind. He stepped forward to the edge of the platform, rapidly clapping his hands to draw the attention of the crowd below him and the watching spirits. He then leaped into the empty space before him. This is Pentecost.

The island of Pentecost was first discovered by Europeans on May 22, 1768, Pentecost Sunday, so explorer Louis Antoine de Bougainville christened it after the holiday. It is a long, narrow island, thirty-seven miles long and a little over six miles wide at its thickest point. Altogether, it is only 189 square miles. It is divided by a row of tortuous mountains along its length. The highest is Mount Vulmat, which is just over three thousand feet high. This mountainous spine creates a wet, rainy east coast and a temperate west coast. Innumerable streams and rivers cut into the sides of the mountains, and waterfalls abound.

The majority of Pentecost's seventeen thousand people live in villages scattered along the west coast. However, there are also notable villages both in the high mountainous interior and on the humid east coast. The people of Pentecost are broken into four language groups—Raga to the north, Apma in the center, Ske in the southwest, and Sa in the south.

Pentecost's primary claim to fame is the ancient ritual of *naghol*, or land diving. In this ritual, each spring, young men climb hillside towers up to one hundred feet high and dive off with only vines tied around their ankles to break their fall. The primary purpose of this rite is to offer a symbolic sacrifice to the spirits that are believed to control the yam harvest. The diver seeks to brush his head against the ground at the bottom of his descent, almost, but not quite, giving his life. A successful dive also comes with significant prestige.

The modern sport of bungee jumping is believed to derive from this ancient ceremony. It is also the subject of a humorous commercial for the Selective Service, though it erroneously identified the ceremony as being from Papua New Guinea.

We have designated the island of Pentecost, along with Santo and Tanna, as one of the focal points of our ministry in Vanuatu. Why? The majority of the people of Pentecost, like most Ni-Vanuatu, identify themselves as Christians. In the south, most villages are Catholic. In the north, most of the villagers would identify themselves as Anglican, and in the central area, most villagers attend a Church of Christ church, which is significantly different from its American counterpart. However, in the south-central, southwest, and north-central areas of Pentecost, a significant number of villages still have no church of any kind.

These pre-Christian communities are our focus. It is in these villages high in the cloud-wrapped mountains of central Pentecost that we long to hear God's praises sung. Instead of offering themselves in a symbolic sacrifice to an ambiguous yam spirit that the men of Pentecost would offer themselves as a living sacrifice to the Eternal God. That instead of trusting themselves to frail vines they would cast themselves upon the mercy of Christ.

But You Never Came

I am standing before a small lady. She is maybe five feet tall. She sports more of a beard and moustache than most fifteen-year-old boys. Her hair is uncombed. Her dress is tattered and stained. She has the round, well-earned shape of a grandmother who bore nine children. But she is not just any grandmother. She is the village matriarch. Every member of that small village can trace their linage through her womb. Her eyes are clear, there are no tears there, but grief shadows them. Her lips tremble, and her hand flutters around her mouth like a butterfly trying to decide on which flower to alight. One sentence flows from her lips over and over again like water spilling over the stones of a brook, *"Bae yu neva bin kam."* "But you never came, you never came."

I don't remember the details of the day. A typical day would start at 5:30 a.m. and extend well into the evening. Often I visit the sick in the hospital, conduct a children's crusade, and teach ministry by example. Upon returning home that evening, I was greeted by my wife, a warm supper, and enthusiastic kids. It was good to be home.

As we prepared to have supper, my wife relayed a message. "A woman came to the house today and asked you to come and pray for her daughter."

"Do you know the woman's name?" I asked.

"No, but I think she's the one in the picture," she replied.

Once we sorted out which picture, I knew who she was talking about—the village matriarch of Pilion. "What's wrong with her daughter?" I asked.

"She didn't say."

"Where is her daughter?"

"I couldn't understand what she was saying," my wife replied.

I knew the daughter. She was around thirty years old and in and out of a local church. The next day I talked with her pastor. "Yes, she is sick," he said. "Yes, the church is looking after her." Yes, I've gone and prayed for her."

With my mind at ease, I delved into my day. I had passing thoughts of her throughout the day. I considered when I might go pray with her, how I would find the house where she was staying, what words of encouragement I would share. But as surely as grains of sand are lost to the wind, my best intentions were lost to my busyness. By the end of the day my thoughts were with my wife, a warm supper, and my children.

The months passed, and that mother's request lay buried in the back of my mind, forgotten and unfulfilled. As I stood to preach at my own grandmother's funeral in Lancaster, Texas, that mother's daughter breathed her last, slipping into eternity. Was she ready? I don't know. Would God have healed her? I can't be sure. Was that mother's heart broken? Did she feel betrayed, forgotten by her missionary? Of that I am certain.

Today, I stand before that mother. I think I will always hear her words. They started as a torrent, then subsided to a whisper, speaking of untold grief, they echo yet, *"Bea yu neva bin kam, yu neva bin kam."*

As missionaries, we are daily troubled by suffering around us. We can easily feel overwhelmed and insufficient. If we are not careful, we will let that sense become our excuse to avoid the suffering of others. But Jesus said, "'Simon son of John, do you truly love me?' He answered, 'Yes, Lord, you know that I love you.' Jesus said, 'Take care of my sheep'" (John 21:16, NIV).

So with a prayer for forgiveness whispered heavenward, I prepare to start again, to tend his sheep.

Hungry Devils

"Oh, this is a good one," I heard from the other side of the curtain. I stood in a makeshift clinic in Ponmuili, a village in south-central Pentecost, translating for Dr. Yumi from Health Care Ministries. We treated patients that still lived in Stone Age conditions. Spending time with doctors and nurses has taught me that when a medical professional refers to a case as a "good one," it is rarely good for the patient. In fact, a good case will often turn your stomach.

The patient presented with a thumb half gnawed off; what remained was swollen, discolored, and oozing pus. Alecia, our daughter, was conducting registration for the clinic and thus was the first to see him. When she asked why he needed to see the doctor, his only answer was to wave his half-eaten thumb under her nose. She decided that was reason enough and bumped him to the front of the line for triage.

The nurse in triage stared speechless at the mangled digit. This was no accident: the thumb had not been cut, crushed, or broken. It was clearly half eaten. She prepared an antiseptic bath and soaked the thumb in preparation for cleaning.

"What happened to your thumb?" the nurse asked.

"A devil ate it," the man nonchalantly replied.

Kara, one of our missionary associates, who was translating, assumed she had misunderstood, so she repeated her question more slowly this time. The man answered more slowly, trying to make this obtuse foreigner understand what he thought should have been obvious just from a quick look at his thumb. "While I was sleeping, a devil came and ate my thumb."

For us Westerners, the idea of a devil causing someone physical harm is ridiculous. Many of us reject the idea of the spiritual entirely; others may believe but cleanly distinguish between the physical and spiritual realms and insist that they do not mingle. A devil may tempt or discourage you, but it cannot eat your thumb.

Yet for Ni-Vanuatu, the physical and spiritual realms are tightly interwoven. The spiritual does impact the physical world. A verbal swear has a real physical result. And devils do get hungry.

A commonly feared type of devil here on Santo is the *patua*; these devils prowl the night sky looking for unsuspecting victims. The hoot of an owl, a rooster crowing at the moon, and even the rustle of a rat on the thatch roofing are interpreted as the approach of a patua. These devils swoop down on the sleeping, eat their intestines, and then stuff their body cavities with leaves or grass. The unsuspecting victim gets up the next morning unaware that he is a walking dead man. He falls suddenly ill, and passes away in spite of any incantations by a local witchdoctor or ministrations by Western-trained medical professionals.

This view is reinforced by local doctors and nurses. Workers at the regional hospital fear being held responsible for the death of their patients. When it appears certain that a patient will die, a nurse will take the family aside and quietly confide that the doctors have determined it is not a medical issue but a spiritual one. They have gone so far as to claim that when doing an autopsy, they have discovered the deceased's abdominal cavity to be stuffed with leaves. The grieving family nods knowingly; clearly there was nothing the hospital could have done.

So what did happen to this man's thumb? Half of the answer is found in kava, the local drug of choice. A strong hypnotic found in the roots of the kava plant induces feelings of peace and tranquility when ingested. It also causes its users to fall into a deep, trancelike sleep. There have been fatalities in Vanuatu from men falling into a kava stupor in the middle of the road; there they peacefully sleep through flying traffic, the squeal of brakes, and blaring horns until someone hits them. A man with enough kava in his system can sleep for days undisturbed—even if something or someone is eating his thumb.

The second half of the equation is rats, an epidemic in Vanuatu. Other than the island boa constrictor and house cats, rats have no natural enemies here. Since Ni-Vanuatu are afraid of snakes and find cats very tasty, the rats pretty much have free reign over the place. Rats are everywhere; they are unafraid of humans and bloodthirsty. More than one night, I have awoken in a village to find huge rats scampering in the rafters overhead or scurrying beside me on the floor.

Recently, a young missionary couple received a fledgling parrot as a present. They were delighted with the bird and pampered it like a child. However, they made the mistake of leaving it unattended in the hut where they had been sleeping while they went outside to eat supper. They returned to the hut to find a group of twenty cat-sized rats fighting over the bloody remains of their parrot. They were stunned to find the rats brazenly refuse to be shooed away from their prize. I don't think the couple slept much that night.

Brazen, bloodthirsty rats explain why many Ni-Vanuatu wash their hands after eating, not before: going to bed with the smell of food on your fingers can be dangerous. This is why babies always sleep with their mothers; it is not a matter of convenience but of protection. It also explains why food is suspended on strings from the rafters over a smoking fire; it is the only way to keep it safe.

A local pastor came in and took one look at the patient's thumb. "Ah, he ate something oily like tuna fish and then fell into a kava stupor. The rats smelled the oil and came and ate his thumb. The kava kept him from waking up." He took the patient aside and began to explain to him that the devil hadn't come to steal his thumb but his soul.

The Lord's Supper

Every prospective missionary dreams of what they will do once they reach the field. When pastoring a small struggling church in the Ozarks before I entered missionary service, I would often dream of fulfilling my call in the Pacific Islands. Instead of looking out over a too-small congregation in a too-large building, I would close my eyes and imagine where I would be. Your heart is always where God has called you, regardless of your physical location.

In my dreams, I imagined planting a church on a remote and largely forgotten island. The services would be held in an open-air tabernacle just off the beach. The view from the pulpit would be eager faces of new converts framed by coconut fronds, white sand, rolling waves, and cool ocean breezes. The setting sun would paint the scattered clouds every color from auburn to fuchsia. The choir would sing "How Great Thou Art" in the local dialect, and I would prepare to serve them Holy Communion for the first time in the history of this fledgling church.

While serving as a missionary in Vanuatu, I have had the privilege of planting churches on remote and largely forgotten islands. Somehow the imagery has never worked out quite the way I dreamed. While many of the settings for these churches have been gorgeous—colossal spreading banyan trees and green-robed mountains soaring into the clouds or plunging into deep blue seas. Temperatures in the high nineties, humidity nudging 100 percent, the conspicuous absence of cool sea breezes, and myriad biting insects, all distract from the natural beauty. I have yet to teach "How Great Thou Art" to a new church and don't know if I ever will.

This Sunday I was preaching in a small white chapel in the village of Nambualou. The service started with the women's side of the building full and the men's side empty. The chief's wife explained that the previous evening the village had celebrated Bonna Annie, a New Year's tradition that involves singing and dancing late into the night. The men, she said, "had too much celebration." I didn't even want to ask what she meant by that. I was preaching here because of problems in the church. The local leadership sometimes used the missionary as a firefighter, so "too much celebration" was, I feared, a phrase pregnant with meaning.

As the service got underway, the men's side slowly began to fill. Bees buzzed lazily in and out of the open windows, crying babies made hearing and understanding nearly impossible, and an oppressive heat began to build. As I took to the pulpit to preach, a little girl dragged a metal-tipped umbrella over the rough cement floor, drowning out my words. Sweating women sat crowded together and beat out a steady rhythm with coconut frond fans, and men who had had too much celebration spread their arms out along the tops of the pews, tipped their heads back, and fell into a deep slumber while babies wailed and urinated on the front steps of the church. Hardly the romantic setting I had envisioned!

Over the course of the sermon, someone relieved the little girl of the umbrella, the babies and their mothers made their way outside to the shade of a nearby tree, a few of the men woke up, and it began to feel a bit more like church. The heat continued to build throughout the sermon, and I watched as our newly arrived missionary associates turned first red and then pale white in the heat. By the time I finished, my shirt was crusted with salt from excessive perspiration.

After the sermon, I prepared to lead the church in taking the Lord's Supper. I looked down at the table before me. The sacraments, some broken vanilla wafers and a watery imitation of grape Kool-Aid, were covered with the only white cloth the church had. I think it had been stolen from some baby's crib, as it was quilted, the edges were trimmed with lace, and a furry bunny was perched in the middle of the fabric. The men who should have dispensed the sacraments were absent, so I had to draft two of the women to serve the congregation.

In that moment I found myself wanting to close my eyes and dream about an air-conditioned church with padded pews, gold-plated communion service, faithful deacons, and the true fruit of the vine in the communion cup.

I kept my eyes open, however, and waited till the women had served the congregation. A hush fell over the church. I opened my Bible, the first Bislama Bible I had ever received. Its pages were marked and dog eared, the binding was beginning to fail, and the front cover had nearly fallen off. I began to read from 1 Corinthians 11:23, *"Tok ya mi mi kasem long Masta blong yumi, mo mi bin talem aot long yufala finis."* ("For I have received of the Lord that which also I delivered unto you."). Tears began to roll down my checks.

No, the setting was not what I had envisioned. No, there was no sudden cooling breeze. But I began to think about the saints that had read these words and participated in this sacrament from the time of the Apostles. I thought of how Christians of all nations and all twenty-four time zones would be hearing those words in thousands of languages, holding a fragile bit of bread in one hand and a trembling cup in the other.

I saw before me not a tired, sweaty group of villagers, but members of his body—part of the enormous organic group that spanned from when the Master broke bread with his disciples on the night of his death till now, two thousand years later, on a small South Pacific island forgotten by most of the world. We joined the global fellowship and continued together to remember and proclaim the Lord's death till he comes again.

Words of Life

What kind of church name is High Cliff Assembly? I wonder. It is a bright Sunday morning, and I am on my way to Louital for a morning service. I am sitting on the nose of a bright yellow, eighteen-foot-long fiberglass boat. We are moving slowly because although our boat could reasonably hold five men, we have close to twenty men, women, and children aboard. The women are dressed for church in brightly colored island dresses with lots of frills and lace; add to these splashes of color the children's insistent chatter and laughter, and it is almost like we are an overcrowded boat of brightly colored riotous parrots.

The sea, rolling gently, remains in pointed contrast to the turmoil in the boat. Its surface is smooth. The water below us is glassy clear, but its color varies with depth, from deep indigo to the lightest aqua. We glide over brilliant mounds of coral of every shape and description. Parrot fish of green, blue, purple, and yellow dash under us, while myriad other tropical fish of every color and hue cluster around the corals on the sea floor.

To my left are soaring limestone cliffs pockmarked with caves and smaller holes. Above the cliff faces, mountains stand with their shoulders wrapped in a thick cloak of tropical foliage while their treeless grassy peaks reach into a lightly clouded sky. Tanna Island is a beautiful place with a complex history. One part of this history holds my thoughts this morning: blackbirding.

In the 1800s, Australian sugar plantation owners looking for a source of cheap labor turned a greedy eye to Vanuatu. The young men were "recruited" to work the plantations, but once they boarded the ships for Australia, they were placed in chains. After years of forced labor, those who survived were returned to Vanuatu. Limited care was given to returning the workers to their correct home islands, a practice that led to many returning workers' being slaughtered and cannibalized on the beach. This practice of kidnapping and forced labor is known as "black birding."

It is appalling that "Christian" people would engage in such barbaric practices. As I mull over the tragedy that changed the face of this island, I wonder if there are any positive stories out of the ashes. Little did I know that the answer was waiting for me at High Cliff Assembly.

After two hours, our parade of color and noise pulls under an imposing cliff face, our landing area consists of huge slabs of stone larger than houses that have fallen off the cliff above us. They lie askew like giant dominoes scattered by the hand of an angry god. The sea rises and falls on one of these half-submerged slabs, and we time our departure from the boat carefully so as to have semidry footing when we emerge onshore. Once on dry land, we make our way between these monoliths to sheer, vertical rock. "Where to now?" I ask.

"Up there, Missionary!" As I crane my head, I see a group of enthusiastic children waving to me several hundred feet above me. "Where," I ask, "is the path?" It turns out that the path is literally straight up the face of the cliff; there are even a couple of ladders composed of saplings tied together with vines. Along the way, we rest in a cave, and I hear stories of expectant mothers who didn't make it all the way down to the boat and gave birth here. I shudder to think of a woman in the eighth or ninth month of pregnancy navigating this cliff, but it is the only way to get to the clinic and midwife several hours away.

After the morning service I am installed on a mat under a shade tree so the chief can tell me the history of this place. "When missionaries first came to this place, it was not planned. They were on their way to the mission compound at Lauwanpakel when they were surprised to see a man in a sulu standing on the shore. It was so unusual in those days to see anyone wearing clothes that they pulled the boat in close to shore to try and talk with the man. When they approached, he pulled out a Bible written in the language of Tonga and began to read it to them. That man was my great-grandfather."

That man, I learned in the course of his story, was a victim of blackbirding. He was kidnapped from Tanna, but the ship he was on sailed to Tonga in search of further victims before returning to Australia. While the ship was anchored in Tonga he escaped his bonds, jumped overboard, and made it to shore. In Tonga, he was taken in by the king, who took a personal interest in him. He was taught to read and write, introduced to the custom of wearing clothes, and led to know Jesus Christ.

"It was my great-grandfather, who escaped from blackbirders, who first brought the gospel to this place."

I can only imagine the wonder of those first missionaries. They were coming to a place of complete darkness. They expected to be greeted only with hostility. Yet there at the base of a cliff, standing among those massive stones, was their Cornelius, prepared by God in advance, a vanguard of the gospel, his legs spread wide against the wind, a Tongan Bible held before him, speaking the Words of Life.

Like Joseph of old, "You intended to harm me, but God intended it for good."

Brace

Seeing the look on the captain's face, I brace myself.

I am sitting on the four-inch side rail of a banana boat; my back is against the house that provides a small sheltered area at the bow, and my feet are wedged against a cross brace on the deck. A wall of water washes over me. I shake my head vigorously to clear my face of streaming seawater so I can catch my breath.

The boat races up a towering wave, twists to avoid capsizing as we broach the crest, springs free, and falls to a bone-jarring crash in the trough between the waves. My stomach, refusing to follow the wild gyrations of the boat, lingers there in the open space above my head. *I never get seasick*, I remind myself.

My stomach and brain conspire against me, filling me with waves of dizziness and nausea. Remembering the advice that I have given to others, I try to focus on an unmoving object so that my brain can process the scrambled signals my inner ears are sending it. I vainly try to focus on nearby Tanna Island, an anchor of stability in a wind-tossed ocean, but alas, all I can see are towering gray mountains of saltwater wearing frothy white caps and, above me, an equally gray and foreboding sky.

A wave slams into the side of the boat even as we prepare to crest the next monster in front of us. "Please God, couldn't you make the waves all come from one direction today?" I pray. The nose of the boat is pointed up, yet we rock violently to the side under the onslaught of this second wave.

The dance of the boat resembles a corkscrew rather than a rocking horse. Ten feet from me at the back of the boat is my good friend, Dick Joel Peter; he is soaked through and water is streaming down his face, which is lit up in a wild grin. *"Woo Huu, Misnari, Tede yumi mekesave ol fis!"* he yells. "All right, Missionary, today we are slaughtering the fish!" He is having fun!

The bottom of the boat is littered with yellow fin tuna that range from ten to fifteen pounds. I try to count them, but by the time I get to twenty my head is spinning. Another wave washes over me, and I stare in amazement as gallons of clear seawater are instantly tainted bloodred. I lift my gaze from the bloody, fish-strewn deck and search for Tanna again. Just as I catch a glimpse of smoking Mount Yasur, I am greeted by my reel screaming as yet another fish strips off the line. "Oh, God," I pray, "please not another one. Please, Lord, help this not to be a big one." My back and rear are battered and bruised by the constant pounding from the waves, my stomach is still playing catch-up from a few waves ago, and my arms are sore from pulling in fish.

If this were my boat, I would never have left shore. The wind is too strong, and the waves too high. For me, fishing is mostly a pleasure activity. Suffering as I catch fish is not my idea of pleasure. I would have taken one look at the surf and forgotten about fishing. If this were my boat, we would have headed for home already, three hundred pounds of yellowfin tuna will fill up my freezer for quite a while, thank you. "Don't be greedy," is my motto.

Clearly this is not my boat. We are fishing to feed a group of over thirty pastors that have come together for a time of spiritual retreat. Pastor Dick and I assigned ourselves the "ministry" of fishing, but I am starting to question the wisdom of my judgment.

In answer to my prayers for a small fish, a five-foot-long mahi mahi breaks the surface, its blue, green, and silver hues muted by the overcast sky. The thought of fighting that size of fish while struggling to contain the contents of my stomach is just too much. I'm finished. I hand the rod to Toupa, who has been working as deckhand. "He's all yours," I tell him. "I'm wiped."

I move to the center of the boat and stand facing the waves; seeing what is coming has always helped me to overcome any pangs of motion sickness. I spot a flock of birds diving into the water for fish and yell for the captain to change course. As we top the last wave before catching up with the birds, the sun breaks through the clouds changing everything.

The wave in front of us is transformed from a foreboding gray to a stunning blue, and the sunlight flashes off a brilliant streak of color racing through the water. It is a bull of a mahi mahi; brilliant blue, green, yellow, and silver all blaze through the wave in front of us. It feels like I could reach out and touch him. His mouth is agape as he crashes through a school of bait fish, and a screaming seabird seizes the opportunity and darts down to snatch bait fish virtually out of his mouth.

Seconds later, the reel screams again, and we pull in what will be our third mahi mahi for the day. It was hours before we returned to shore with hundreds of pounds of fish, but in my mind, that day will always be defined by that one moment.

The sun, shining on brilliantly blue water, a million diamonds sparkling off the waves, and there under the glassy surface, a bull mahi mahi, mouth agape, gills flared, colors blazing, bait fish frantically darting away in hope of escape, and a seabird fixed there in the air, his scream echoing off the water, his bill slicing through the wave and preparing to steal the mahi mahi's last meal.

Bind Up the Broken Hearted

I am sitting on a bench crafted from massive bamboo in the middle of a village in South Santo. There is a festive spirit in the air. Little kids race in circles, sporting bright crayon-colored flags tied or taped to sticks or short bits of bamboo. A generator has been fired up, speaker wires are strung, and a makeshift sound system blares out music with a lively beat. Teenagers flirt and tease one another; groups of girls and knots of boys move back and forth in the village green, accidentally, intentionally intersecting and colliding and then separating to a chorus of embarrassed giggles. Today starts the beginning of a week-long celebration of Vanuatu's thirtieth anniversary of independence. Everybody should be happy, but the man sitting beside me is weeping with deep, heart-wrenching sobs.

This village, Nomoro, was one of the first villages in South Santo to have an Assembly of God church. The initial Bible studies I held here were met with hostility and threats. New believers, afraid for their well-being, fled the village. Today the anger and fear have subsided, and the new church has been accepted. The majority of the villagers would not think of attending, but open persecution has stopped. Several of the initial converts went on to attend classes at the Sanma Bible Training Center and then planted their own churches in neighboring villages. Four churches have sprung up from what was originally a hostile environment. I think this history makes today an even more painful day.

Three weeks ago I received a phone call. "Missionary, we have a problem in Nomoro." It seems that Jon, one of our former students, one that had shown great potential, had propositioned the wife of another young man who was away at Bible school in Port Vila. When she declined, he threatened to rape her, but thankfully he was interrupted by a passerby before he could carry through with his threat.

I found myself angry at many levels. Angry at a young man who had betrayed his wife, his children, and his former classmate. I wanted to shake him and ask him, "Why?" I was angry at a system of Bible schools that required men to leave their wives and children for three years at a time if they wanted to prepare themselves for ministry. I wanted to shake leadership for consistently failing to build married student housing and ask them, "Why?" I was angry at Satan for the heartache and havoc he loved to wreak on homes.

This morning we made our way down the dirt road to Nomoro. Our Speed the Light truck danced and shook its way around, through, and over potholes of amazing depth and width. An enormous plume of white dust rose behind the truck, coating the foliage beside the road with yet another thin film of dirt. We parked and walked down the muddy trail off of the road that leads to the church house at Nomoro. There we were welcomed by Pastor Samson and the church. After the service, Pastor Samson comes to sit with me.

"Where is Jon?" I ask.

"Missionary, I am glad you have come. You need to talk with him. Since I disciplined him, he has not come back to church."

We make our way to Pastor Samson's kitchen for a meal of yam laplap, tinned meat, grapefruit, and bananas. While the ladies prepare the meal, I walk over to the bamboo bench beside the village green. I tell a young boy that I want to see Jon and settle down to wait. Soon, a quiet young man slips onto the bench beside me. His head is down, eyes averted. Eye contact would be too painful.

One of the many differences between America and Vanuatu is the use of tone in communication. Most communication in Vanuatu occurs in a very quiet tone of voice. What would be a normal tone of voice in America means one of two things in the context of Vanuatu; what is being said is in jest or the speaker is very angry. Many Americans are never taken seriously here, and others have Ni-Vanuatu trembling in fear every time they speak. Needless to say, Vanuatu is a very challenging place for those who are hard of hearing. Today, I want Jon to know I am deadly serious but I don't want to convey anger, so I whisper in an almost inaudible tone.

Truthfully, anger is what I feel. The longer I am in ministry, the more appreciation I have for the words of Christ in Matthew 5:6, "Blessed are those who hunger and thirst after righteousness." (NIV) All my life I have heard preachers construe this passage to mean we should hunger and thirst after God, as we should, but that is not what Christ said, he said righteousness. Sin mars lives, destroys futures, wrecks homes, devastates ministries, and robs individuals of human dignity. I hate sin. A person is blessed if they hunger and thirst after righteousness.

When faced with a situation like Jon's or another where a father had beaten and raped his own daughter, I am angry. I want to shake the person and say, "How could you have been so stupid? Don't you see how this ruins your ministry? Don't you see how you have hurt your wife? Don't you see how you have crushed your daughter?" For a minute, in my human weakness, I wish that they could get what they deserve. But God doesn't want this, not even for a moment.

God paid an awful price just so we wouldn't get what we deserve. I have had to deal with far too many such cases where a man of God was caught in open sin. Yet in each case I have found the Spirit leading me to Romans 5:8, "While we were yet sinners, Christ died for us." (KJV)

"Jon," I whisper, "Christ didn't die for good men. He died for sinners."

While inwardly my spirit rages that such men should be punished, the Holy Spirit reveals them to me as torn and ravaged by sin. Yes, their sin wounded others; deep wounds that will ache for a lifetime. Yet, at the same time, it maimed them. They lay broken like the man on the road to Jericho. I hear the Spirit whisper to me, "Bind up the broken hearted."

The Table of Demons

"Missionary, I don't reject the church. I hold the church in one hand and my culture in the other," the chief said to me as he tried to explain why he didn't want the spirits removed from his *nasara*, a tribal meeting area where he resolved disputes. "One of my grandfathers was a paramount chief, and the other was the first pastor in my tribe. I hold both the church and my culture as my heritage."

The ocean between Santo and Aore islands was calm and smooth. The water parted effortlessly before the bow of the boat. Our wake spread out behind us in an ever-expanding V, gently rocking multimillion dollar yachts on one side and hand-carved dugout canoes on the other. Enormous schools of sardines clustered in thick balls throughout the channel while marauding tuna, mahi mahi, and karong tore through them, wreaking havoc on the sardines and making the water roil. The pilot of the ferry told me he had been catching tuna all day on a hook decorated with only a flower. The fisherman in me was going insane.

It was Memorial Day, and in an effort to keep our kids in touch with American culture, we had taken the day off to visit a nearby resort where the kids could swim and kayak. Over pizza we discussed the purpose of the holiday and described to our children how our families had traditionally spent the day.

Now the day was finished. Sun, swimming, and too much rich food were taking their toll. On the ferry home, sun-baked faces, more asleep than awake, stared vacantly off toward the blue horizon. A chief that wanted to talk broke my fixation on the fish. "I have two wives," he bragged, "and soon I will get two more."

What kind of missionary would I be if I didn't respond to a statement like that? Polygamy, while not common in Vanuatu, is not unheard of. If a man holds a significant position in the local council of chiefs, the government, or a prosperous business, his taking more than one wife is excused. Because many Ni-Vanuatu consider a marriage to be solemnized when the bride price has been paid and because young brides can be purchased for around eight hundred dollars, many men find themselves in a position where they can have multiple wives. Few, however, are quick to bring up the subject in conversation with a total stranger.

The only reason to make such a provocative statement was to engage in a spirited discussion, and I decided to rise to the bait. For several minutes, we discussed the practical implementation of polygamy. Do you house the two wives together? How do they feel about sharing their husband? How would his current wives feel when he added two more?

He was cocky and confident, assuring me that each of his wives felt privileged to be married to such a high-ranking man and that jealousy was not an issue. I struggled to keep my skepticism from showing on my face. I would have loved to have a private interview with his wives to discover their true feelings on the matter.

He explained that taking multiple wives was a matter of culture. In his tribe, chiefhood was inherited. Even so, a young man did not automatically become a chief; he first had to achieve certain ranks. Each of these ranks were accompanied by certain prerogatives that the community expected the young chief to exercise.

At his current rank, he was entitled to two wives. The next rank, the highest, included the prerogative of taking up to four wives, which he fully intended to do. I ask him which tribe he was from. When he told me he is from the Maskelynes, I commented that the Assemblies of God had recently opened a church on Uleveo, his home island.

He met my announcement with a stony gaze. "I don't believe you, but even if it is true, your church will never last," he tells me. "We are Presbyterians. We have been Presbyterian since the first missionaries came. We are firmly committed to the church, and we would never change."

I was incredulous. "Does the Presbyterian church endorse your polygamy?" I asked.

"No, of course not," he replied. "One is religion; the other is culture. I can hold on to both, but I have to be careful. If I go to church too much I will lose my culture, so I hold my culture higher."

I was amazed. While I knew that syncretism was widely practiced in Vanuatu, I had never had anyone explain the practice to me in such open terms.

Syncretism, as defined by *Encyclopedia Britannica* is "the fusion of diverse religious beliefs and practices." At certain levels, it is an unavoidable consequence of bringing the gospel into pre-Christian cultures. Western culture reflects this; the modern holidays of Christmas, Easter, and Halloween are the heritage of pre-Christian European cultural celebrations that have been "baptized" into Christianity.

My concern is when people hold or attempt to meld two mutually exclusive beliefs. One example would be believing that Christ is the only way to eternal life, yet at the same time just as fervently believing that reproducing a sacred sand drawing is the key to get past the she-demon that guards the entrance to the afterlife.

Another example might be believing that God is all powerful but that some kinds of sickness can only be cured by the *kleva*, the local equivalent of a witchdoctor. The Melanesian propensity to whole-heartedly hold two religious ideas that are diametrically opposed caused one anthropologist to postulate that perhaps Melanesians have two souls.

Truthfully, every culture struggles with syncretism. The gospel preached by many famous American televangelists far more accurately portrays the current American fixation on materialism and moral relativism than the gospel preached by Christ. Christ even rebuked Jewish culture when he said in Mark 7:13, "you nullify the word of God for the sake of your tradition" (NIV).

The ancient Corinthians struggled with this issue as well. The culture and economy of Corinth was dominated by temples. Culturally significant celebrations revolved around meals based on sacrifices. When the chief argued for keeping the spirits that inhabited his nasara in order to deal with issues that in his view were outside the scope of Christianity, I was reminded of Paul's words to the Conrinthians in I Corinthians 10:21: "You cannot drink the cup of the Lord and the cup of demons too; you cannot have a part in both the Lord's table and the table of demons" (NIV).

The answer to syncretism lies in the challenge Joshua posed to the children of Israel, who had publicly worshiped Jehovah while privately maintaining shrines to idols. "Choose you this day whom ye will serve; whether the gods which your fathers served that were on the other side of the flood, or the gods of the Amorites, in whose land ye dwell: but as for me and my house, we will serve the LORD" (Joshua 24:15 KJV).

Rainy Day Missionary

I peered out the door of the tin shack into the misty rain. After a downpour all night, I wasn't sure how long this break would last. I decided to make my way to the kitchen before the leaden skies let loose another deluge. I gathered my Bible and notebook and set off through the mist. The kitchen was a quarter of a mile down a muddy road from my hut. I slowly wove my way around mud puddles, doing my best to avoid drenching my shoes. I failed.

The constant moisture had caused the glue holding the rubber soles of my shoes to the upper to lose its grip, starting at the toes. The gap made my shoes look like a wide grin was slowly spreading across their face. As I made my way along the muddy road, they beat out a steady tattoo: the suction of the mud held my sole for just a moment after I had raised my foot, and once the sole sprang free, from the mud's embrace it slapped the leather bottom of the upper before setting down with a splat on the muddy road again. Slap, splat; slap, splat. As I trudged along, the action of the sole splattered bits of mud from the hem of my pants up to the knee. Nothing like arriving in style.

I slogged across the muddy field, where three hundred people had stood in the rain for yesterday evening's service, that bordered the kitchen and dining area. The kitchen was a thatch hut, its steeply pitched roof ending in eaves that brushed the ground. Inside women labored over boiling pots that rested on smoky fires. The rain-soaked wood smoldered and sputtered, and a thick haze of smoke and steam filled the kitchen and seeped out from the open ends of the roof, curling lazily into the still air.

The dining area was a high bar, long and narrow and covered by a small thatch roof that was only a hair wider than it. A couple of pastors and I squeezed against the bar on one side, pressing against it to keep our backs from brushing against the dripping palm fronds hanging from the edge of the thatch. We ate our rice and sipped our coffee and mused about the weather. Surely the sun would at least make an appearance.

Later, I left the dining area and climbed into the small hut that the pastors from across Tanna were using as sleeping quarters. The hut had been built on stilts to provide some relief from the mud. The floor and walls were of woven bamboo. The floor was covered with sleeping mats and blankets, and there was barely space between them to place my feet. The construction of the floor was questionable. With each step the bamboo would groan and dip under my weight till I was sure that my foot would plunge through. Gingerly, I made my way to the side of the hut where I could sit with my back against a post.

I leaned back against my post and let my eyes follow the steep angle of the thatch roof above me. Its woven palm fronds had aged to a chestnut brown. The rafters, slender saplings stripped of their bark, provided a pleasing contrast to the thatch, and vines tied each section of thatch to them. It was incredibly primitive, yet homey. The thatch was amazing in its ability to withstand the tropical downpours.

Seated around me are the pastors—Pastor Joni, an overweight man in his forties who could climb mountains without ever stopping to catch his breath; Pastor Obed, whose house and church had been burned three times in attempts to run him out of his village, who always remained chipper and upbeat, thrilled to tell you a new story of what God is doing every time you saw him; and Pastor Jimmy, a high-ranking chief who could easily have lived a life of comfort in his own village, but instead pioneered one new church after another in some of the most difficult places on Tanna.

We had agreed to meet this morning for a training session for altar workers and counselors. More pastors gathered, and soon there were fifteen of us in the hut, which measured no more than ten by twenty feet. We opened with prayer. I spread my Bible and notes out on the floor before me and taught for the next hour. During the course of my teaching, the clouds burst. When our scheduled time together had come to an end, each of us looked out the door into the pouring rain. Morning Bible classes, door-to-door evangelism, and literature distribution had been planned for that day. Instead, we decided that staying inside the dry hut and having some coffee was the best option.

Two of the pastors braved the storm to fetch coffee cups, instant coffee, and a pot of boiling water. As I mixed my first cup of coffee, one of the pastors spoke up. "Missionary, would you mind if I asked you a couple of questions?"

I sat cross-legged on the floor well into the afternoon. Rain steadily drummed on the thatch above us. Slowly nursing cups of coffee, I answered questions with an open Bible. The questions were far ranging, and each one provoked more. We discussed everything from the pastors' marriages to questions concerning the Sabbath. The pastors thumbed through well-worn Bibles, underlining passages and taking notes. No, this was not what I had planned for today, but this was some of the most effective ministry a missionary could ever engage in. Ministry like this comes only after you have invested the time necessary to master your host culture and language, often years, and is born out of trust and relationship.

This is what it means to be a Rainy Day Missionary.

Small Bryan

The Pongo churchyard, the grass neatly mowed, was decorated with flowers. Tents spread out along the perimeter, and blue plastic chairs had been arranged in rows in front of the church. Tonight was graduation night for Joy Bible Institute. I arrived early so I could visit with the graduates and pastors that I rarely got to see. I was especially delighted to see Pastor Peter Solomon and his wife come through the gate.

Ten months ago, Pastor Peter had asked me to pray with him and his wife that they would be able to have a child. Two months ago, Pastor Peter contacted me to say that his wife was seven months pregnant. I joyfully congratulated him and playfully suggested that if the child was a boy, the couple should name him after me.

There are lots of "Small Bryans" around Vanuatu. Naming your child after the missionary is a common practice. The original "Small Bryan" was our son; small was the term the Ni-Vanuatu used to distinguish him from his father. Time has erased that distinction for my son, since he now borders on six feet tall, the term "Small Bryan" doesn't quite fit anymore. However, once you have a label, getting rid of it is no simple matter.

A Small Bryan has gotten me into trouble. While visiting the village of Vinmavis with a pastor friend from the States, I was introduced to one of my namesakes. In Bislama, an elder explained to me that a child had been born the day after my last visit, so his parents named him after me. Of course, my pastor friend was oblivious to this conversation. Hours later, as we ate supper, the same elder made an announcement in English. "You remember your last visit here?" he asked. "This is Small Bryan," he said as he ushered a young boy before us. My pastor friend nearly choked on his chicken. I can only imagine what conclusions he drew from this exchange.

I thought it prudent to clarify. "Ah," I said, "you mean the one who was born the day after I visited last time?"

Tonight I was eager to meet who I hoped would be the next Small Bryan. Pastor Peter and his wife, dear friends, had waited seven years since the birth of their daughter, praying and believing that God would give them a son. Numerous miscarriages punctuated their wait. As I walked across the well-groomed churchyard, I anticipated the feel of a newborn in my arms. Boys or girls, babies are fun.

I greeted them with a huge smile. "Where is Small Bryan?" I asked. Immediately, I knew I had made a tragic mistake. Grief and pain lined both of their faces.

"Missionary, I feel like Job," Pastor Peter told me. "The Lord has given to us, but he has also taken away. Our son was born on Tuesday, but it was a difficult birth. He passed away on Thursday. We never even heard him cry. We buried him two days ago."

I listened in shock as they described the breach birth. The father said that he repeatedly begged the doctor to perform a cesarean birth, only to have his pleas fall on deaf ears. The mother described the agony of the baby being stuck in the birth canal and the knowledge that every minute he was stuck endangered her child further, yet she was unable to deliver. The baby was born unresponsive, and although the doctor was able to get him to start breathing, he never cried, and he never nursed. He was placed in an incubator, and the parents never had the opportunity to hold him while he lived. Three days later, he was gone.

"Missionary, I tried and tried to call you, but I could never get through. It felt like the line to heaven had been cut." I realized that at the time he was trying to contact me, I was with a group of American medical professionals ministering on Pentecost Island, outside cell phone service. How I wish now that I could have gotten that call and joined with them in prayer for a miracle.

The injustice of it hit me hard. In America, a fetal heart monitor would have signaled that the baby was struggling, and an emergency caesarian would have been moments away. I know this because our first child was breach and in danger. I remember watching in stunned silence as what had seemed like a normal delivery suddenly turned into an emergency surgery. I remember the first cries of that baby girl as the doctor lifted her into the brightly lit operating room. What separates me and my family from Pastor Peter and his loss? The accident of birth—I was born in America, he in Vanuatu.

I wept with Pastor Peter and his wife and wished I had words that would take away the pain. I could only ask that my Father bear them up in his arms, comfort their hearts with his love, numb the pain with his peace, and give them the strength to stand by his grace. By his grace, they would be able to echo the words of Job, "the LORD gave, and the LORD hath taken away; blessed be the name of the LORD." Job 1:21 KJV

Next time I pass this way, I will purchase a tombstone for Small Bryan.

Ranpator

The beach beneath your feet is course and irregular. It requires a ginger step, for it is far too rough for tender feet. A pebble beach, it consist of pieces really too big to be called pebbles, yet too small to be stones. Its color is gray with fragments of whitewashed coral from the sea and smooth black stones from the hills. When you sit down and take the time to examine it closely, you find pieces of red that glow in the setting sun. There are bits of green you swear are emeralds. Round black stones are marbled with lines of sparkling quartz, and crushed shells of giant clams yield shimmering iridescent oblique chunks that would tempt you to believe you had found a diamond. Here a bit of fire coral has maintained its deep red hue; there a broken seashell lies half hidden among the pebbles, deceiving you into thinking you have found the perfect souvenir. Your fingers linger over a round lump of pumice from a nearby smoking volcano, and you try to savor the remnant of heat from its burning, belching vents.

You could spend a lifetime just studying the components of the beach, but peals of far-off laughter from children cause you to lift your eyes and follow the line of beach to the north. This same beach stretches out in a wavering line as far as your eye can see till it is lost in the curve of the island. Palm trees lazily stretch out over it, turning to lift their feather crowns to the sun at the last moment. Hand-hewn canoes sporting deftly carved outriggers are pulled safely above the surf line. There, at the curve, a great green hill rises, its sides clothed with a rich bouquet of tropical flora and its crest topped with a high fringe of coconut palms. It stands bare to the west as if it were longing to wash its stony face in the spray of the breaking waves. The curved bay below rolls with a light swell, yet its surface is smooth without so much as a ripple to break the tension.

There, at the first meandering of the beach, is the group of children whose laughter distracted you. They look like sea nymphs running along the course beach, leaping into the air and performing complete flips before splashing into the surf. Once in the water, the group bobs along in the flowing tide, laughing and chattering away. They dive for stones, disappearing beneath the smooth surface, competing to gather the largest ones. Up again they come, splashing a silvery spray of seawater as they shake their heads to clear their eyes. The water forms perfect beads of dew on their hair, sparkling like a thousand diamonds almost as bright as their eyes. Bored with diving, they chase one another in a frenzied game of tag. Their laughter and screams of delight carry far out over a slumbering ocean.

To the west, the setting sun paints the sky with every hue from crimson to pink. The scattered clouds blush deeply as the sun gilds them lightly. The gently rolling swells reflect the crimson of the sky, mingling it with their own mysterious blues to yield a spectrum of color from lavender to violet to deep scarlet.. Enthroned in this majestic setting, the sun slowly lowers himself toward the horizon like a monarch retiring to an evening of slumber. No longer the brilliant firebrand of the afternoon; he is now a ruddy old gentleman, a great red orb floating in the west. At the moment he touches the horizon, he splashes it with glowing burnt auburn. Then, oh so swiftly, he slips below the horizon, seeming to melt into the waves.

The radiant clouds above infuse the tropical twilight with a soft pink glow. The beach is no longer gray with competing bits of white and black; now it is ruby with bits of coral glowing a soft peach among stones of lustrous burgundy. The smell of woodsmoke pulls your attention from the beach. There, under great spreading nadao trees, a patch has been torn in the carpet of green grass. In the tear, a fire glimmers and winks at you in the gathering twilight. Stretched above the fire, a pig slowly turns on the spit, and you become aware of other smells.

You make your way slowly across the rough coral and stone of the glowing beach before finding the soft comfort of grass. Once on the carpet you can move more quickly, but you don't; you linger to savor this moment. Beside the fire are the fathers of the children you saw earlier. Men with dark skin, beards, and hair, their arms shine in the firelight. Bones wrapped in muscle, sinew, and skin flex and twist to rotate the roasting pig. From the dark shadows of their thickly bearded faces, their eyes shine with laughter and their smiles reveal bright white teeth. The sounds of the Sa language wash over your ears, strangely familiar till you realize their cadence mimics the whisper of the surf on the stones behind you.

You make your way to the side of the fire, and a knife is placed in your hands. As you bend over the roasting pig, the sizzles and pops of hot grease greet you. The aroma of woodsmoke mingles with the rich fragrance of roast pork, and your mouth waters. Your fingers burn as you slice a sizzling strip of meat off the hog. You try to wait for the morsel to cool, but you can't. Hot grease burns your tongue while the tender pork melts in your mouth.

This is Ranpator.

Who Carries Your Mother's Water?

High in the misty mountains of Tanna, the village of Yanemilen sits in the fold of the hill, like a child reclining in the arms of a grandfather. Surrounded by thick, vine-choked jungle, it is an island in time. A mile to the south of the village, Mount Yasur comes and goes as the grey fog slides over it. Like a tired old man, it grunts and grumbles ceaselessly, its complaints occasionally punctuated by a reverberating "Boom!" as it spits clouds of ash and lava kilometers into the sky.

New visitors to the village find the setting mesmerizing. As the sun sets, the sky over Mount Yasur glows a deep red. Explosions boom and echo against the side of the mountain, and with each eruption, lumps of glowing lava spray into the night sky like sparks from a stirred campfire. The nightly show from Mount Yasur, the towering column of ash and steam each day, and the gray wisps of fog slipping through the tangle of the surrounding jungle make Yanemilen a mystical place. It is easy to understand why the villagers have such faith in magic.

Today, though, the villagers have no interest in their vista. Like people everywhere, the beauty that surrounds them quickly becomes mundane. "A volcano spewing lava a mile away? That's nothing! Today there is a family of white people in the village!" Curiosity brightens the eyes of the entire village, and excited chatter spills from every lip. A young missionary couple, Ken and Mindy Nehrbass, have brought their family to live here.

The meeting of two worlds is always filled with fascinating observations. Common kitchen items from America are baffling curiosities to the locals. Electronics are magical. Long, straight, silky blond tresses beg to be stroked, luring the fingers of even the most bashful into touching the foreigner. However, one of the most curious things about the foreigners is the size of the family. Where are the rest of them?

To a Ni-Vanuatu, the nuclear family consists of the father and mother, their adult sons and their wives, and finally their grandchildren. Families are large, noisy, and meant to stay together. Ni-Vanuatu families do separate sometimes, but they almost always view separations as a temporary situation, even when they last a lifetime. It would be fine to leave your family for a visit, but for good?

As Mindy and the women discuss family dynamics, she explains that American adult children leave their parents to start their own homes. Building your own house in your parent's village makes sense, but halfway around the world? One of the women asks her a poignant question: "Who carries your mother's water?"

In Yanemilen, one of life's daily chores is getting water. It means a long trek to a spring and then carting that water back up the hill to the village. Women and young girls carry the bulk of the water since they do the cooking and cleaning. Older arthritic women depend on their daughters-in-law to carry their water. On the surface, the simple answer is to explain with a laugh that all homes in America have running water. However, the woman's question exposes a deeper, more serious issue for missionaries, one that has led to many missionaries' leaving the field: who cares for our aging parents?

This is seldom a concern for new missionaries. The average missionary starts his or her career in the late twenties or early thirties. The pressing issues are homeschooling in a foreign environment and acquiring the local language. At that stage of life, parents are normally still working, healthy, and capable caregivers. However, fifteen to twenty years into a missionary's career, things begin to change. Parents that have always been independent find themselves needing a caregiver. What is a missionary to do?

I will never forget sitting in the oncologist's office with my father a few weeks before our return to the field for our third term. Hearing him reveal that Dad had a very aggressive form of cancer felt like a physical blow. The funds had been raised, the containers were packed, and tickets had been purchased for our journey. It was time to go, but no one wants to abandon parents in their time of need. But go we did. From the far side of the world, we waited anxiously to hear the results of surgeries: heart bypass, cancer removal, hip replacement. Not being there is nearly as difficult as knowing your parents are undergoing such trying times.

What one fears is not death; both of my parents are believers, and I am confident we will be reunited. The worry is that a parent who needs your care will be left alone. Who mows the lawn, paints the house, repairs the car, fixes the leak in the roof, or changes the lightbulbs? Who carries your mother's water?

Divine Placement

The chief's wife bashfully held her hand behind her back. She was a robust woman in her early thirties wearing only a grass skirt and a timid smile. Her grass skirt swished noisily as she nervously shifted her weight from leg to leg. Two bright-eyed preschool girls wearing miniature copies of her skirt clung to her shyly while staring at the strange white women. Elaine, the triage nurse, greeted the girls and their mother with a welcoming smile before focusing on the patient card for the mother. "Cut on right hand," she read. "Can you show me your hand?"

Reluctantly, the woman presented it to Elaine. The bloodstained skin of the palm was split, and fatty tissue from below protruded through the rupture. Clearly she would need stitches. But something about the wound raised questions. "What happened to your hand?" Elaine asked.

The woman's eyes dropped to the floor. She turned her head away from Elaine and her translator and choked out her answer in an almost inaudible whisper: "My husband did it. He hit me with a piece of wood."

Unfortunately, her experience is all too common here in Vanuatu, where wives are purchased. The bride price is eighty thousand vatu, or about eight to nine hundred dollars. Some would argue that this is merely a cultural formality of little consequence; perhaps this is true. All I know is that a wedding I was supposed to perform last week was cancelled at the last minute against the wishes of both the bride and groom because the family of the groom couldn't provide the entire bride price.

The natural consequence of men purchasing their wives is a sense of possession. Women are removed from the ownership of their fathers to the ownership of their husbands. They call their husbands "Papa" just as they have called their fathers. Most Ni-Vanuatu men that I have discussed this issue with insist that it is right and even necessary for men to "discipline" their wives on occasion. I know very few men here who claim they have never struck their wives in anger.

In this culture where women are chattel, where they are often known not by their names but as "woman blong chief," literally "the woman that belongs to the chief," where they have little protection under the law, and where it is the norm for a husband to punish his wife, how do the women feel about this abuse? Is it just expected, a normal part of the marriage relationship? If everyone does it, does a young bride have any honest expectation that it will not happen to her?

The pained explanation from the chief's wife tells me that women here do hope. That in the heart of every woman, regardless of cultural conditioning, is a longing to be cherished and protected. That while their culture and the experiences of their mothers may tell them a story of pain and betrayal, love whispers to their hearts that another narrative is possible, and, in fact, is their right: a story of tenderness, kindness, and security.

Tears roll down Elaine's cheeks and drip from her chin. "I was a battered wife, too," she begins. There in our day clinic with doctors and nurses working by flashlights in the dusky interior of a thatch hut, Elaine tenderly washes the chief's wife's hand and shares her own story. She tells of feelings of sorrow, betrayal, and even coming to believe that somehow she deserved to be abused. As she gently swabs the broken palm, she relates her feelings of hopelessness and her desperate search for true love.

Smiling through her tears, she discloses the healing she has found for a broken heart in the loving arms of Christ. She urges the chief's wife to come to know and accept the love of Christ. "You need to realize just how much God loves you. He sent this team all the way from America just to serve your village. Out of all the nurses here today, God arranged it so you were my patient. He did that because he loves you so much. To let you know that he sees your pain."

I watch the tears drop from the chins of both women and marvel at God's placement once again. A few stitches begin the healing for the broken skin, but an incredible display of God's love began to mend a broken heart.

Christmas Shopping in Vanuatu

The light is dim, filtered through a narrow row of grime-coated windows close to the ceiling. The air is heavy with the pungent aroma of mothballs mixed with body odor. The aisles are narrow and crowded, causing me to brush into merchandise on each side. I make my way through an amazing array of inventory, some of which I am sure dates back at least three decades, while listening to a loud speaker blare out a rendition of "White Christmas" by an island reggae band whose members have never seen snow. I am looking for something, anything really, that would even remotely resemble a Christmas present for a child.

The maze I am in yields miscellaneous plumbing parts, kerosene lanterns, meat grinders, tea towels celebrating New Hebrides (the name for Vanuatu…before independence in1980!), the *Little Red Book* by Chairman Mao, faded school uniforms, broken plastic swords, and cheap Barbie doll replicas whose plastic wrappers have turned orange with time. No, I am not at a flea market or in a junk store; I am standing in the equivalent of Walmart in Santo, affectionately called "Chinese Shops" by locals. Okay, sometimes the affection is missing.

"Oh, look!" Renee says. To see what has caused this excitement, I make my way around a stack of cardboard pictures depicting various scenes of

Chinese village life (I assume they were painted before Chairman Mao wrote his red book) that are water stained and bowed with age. There, hidden behind a concrete column, wrapped in plastic to protect it from the dust, is an honest to goodness teddy bear. He is brown, two feet high, and has almost the correct body proportions.

Each shopper in a Chinese store in Santo is given a personal shopping assistant; well, really a personal security guard that follows you through the store to make sure you don't shoplift any of this valuable stock. They must be doing a good job because this is my first visit to this particular store since last Christmas, and by my observations, no merchandise has moved. These personal shopping assistants take the personal part of their job seriously; it seems that their idea of proper distance for surveillance is three to five inches.

I turn, nearly bumping into my personal shopping assistant, and ask, "How much is the teddy bear?"

"The what?" she replies.

When I point out the bear my wife is looking at, she looks like she has never seen it before, but then, the lighting is very dim.

"I think," she says, "you will have to ask the master."

In this case, "the master" is an overweight Chinese lady in her midforties. Her face badly scarred by acne, she is holding her cigarette with one hand and fighting flies with the other.

"Excuse me," I say. I just can't bring myself to address her or anyone else as master. "How much for the teddy bear?"

"The what?" she grunts, clearly irritated that I have not addressed her by a properly respectful title. I move the plastic-shrouded bear from behind the column into her view.

"Fifty bucks," she spits out. I am desperate but find the price to be extreme, Renee sighs as I return the bear to his place on the shelf.

Christmas shopping in Vanuatu has many of the same frustrations as it does in America. The traffic is terrible; one day I had to wait almost five minutes before I could make a U-turn. The weather is frightful, often over 90 degrees with high humidity. You can never find a parking space— Chinese businessmen don't believe in wasting real estate on parking lots. However, the greatest challenge in Santo is not avoiding the over commercialization of Christmas. No, our challenge is finding something to purchase in the first place.

In a country where hardly anyone can afford anything more than the necessities of life, the stores don't carry a lot of nonessentials. More than one Christmas, our children have awoken to find such surprises as flashlights, hammers, machetes, hatchets, or a case of soft drinks under the Christmas tree. I have, however, refrained from putting cuttlefish-flavored corn puffs in their stockings. Yes, they really do sell such a thing here.

The situation forces us to place our focus for this season where it should be every Christmas—on the miracle of our Savior's birth. This Sunday I gathered our family at the front of the church, and we sang "Hark the Herald Angels Sing." When was the last time you really thought about the words of the song?

> Hark! The herald angels sing, 'Glory to the newborn King;
> Peace on earth and mercy mild; God and sinners reconciled.'
> Joyful, all ye nations rise, Join the triumph of the skies;
> With angelic hosts proclaim, 'Christ is born in Bethlehem.'
>
> Christ, by highest heav'n adored, Christ the everlasting Lord;
> Late in time behold Him come, Offspring of a virgin's womb.
> Veiled in flesh the God-head see, Hail th'incarnate Deity!
> Pleased as man with men to appear, Jesus our Immanuel here.
>
> Hail the heav'n born Prince of Peace, hail the Son of righteousness!
> Light and life to all He brings, Ris'n with healing in His wings:
> Mild He lays His glory by, Born that man no more may die;
> Born to raise the sons of earth, Born to give them second birth.

No, I don't like celebrating Christmas in Vanuatu.

I miss snow, blustery cold winds, blazing fireplaces, cheerful Christmas lights, and mistletoe. I miss turkey, dressing, ham, cranberry sauce, and pecan fudge. I miss clean grocery stores, groceries I can afford, busy shopping malls loaded with options, and lines of children waiting to sit on a fake Santa's lap.

I miss Christmas cantatas, children's Christmas programs, fruit sacks after church, and the "Bless this house" calendars that my pastor always gave out at the last service before Christmas. I miss last-minute runs to the store for Christmas dinner, carving the turkey, laughing with cousins, arguing with nephews, and being with family.

Sometimes I miss it so much it hurts. I grieve that my children will never have the memories that I have. I envy missionaries that serve close to the States and go home for Christmas. Yet I have an incredible privilege. I get to tell people about Christmas who have never heard the story before.

Sunrise Baptism

I step out onto the beach a few minutes before sunrise. The predawn atmosphere is moist from the previous night's rain. The air is filled with the sound of waves breaking; rolling in, stumbling over themselves, and retreating back into the bay. The black sand feels warm and rough on my bare feet. Hot springs bubble up through the sand and fill oceanside tidal pools with scalding water, giving off steam that drifts lazily over the bay. The steam, in turn, infuses the morning with a hint of sulfur. To the west, Mount Yasur rumbles and spits glowing chunks of lava; to the east, the yet unseen sun backlights the coastline, burning the horizon crimson.

It was here on this sandy beach that the gospel first came to Tanna. November 5, 1858, John Paton landed here at Port Resolution. The tree where he tied up his boat still stands. So do the grave stones of early missionary children. The tragedy is that this place, which should be a stronghold of Christianity, is today one of the darkest places in Vanuatu. Early on there was a great acceptance of the gospel, but something changed and the people, led by their chiefs, returned to darkness.

I am standing on this historic beach because of a new church in a village just down the road, the village of Itapu. Over the last week, I have been holding daily services in conjunction with the construction of a church building. Each night as I finish my evening meal, I can hear villagers gathering in the darkness outside of the hut. Children chatter impatiently for the service to start, and mothers hush them. One evening as I eat, a little boy wants to come inside the circle of light thrown by the lamp on the table, and his mother rebukes him, "Leave the tourists alone," she says. I explain that I am decidedly not a tourist and that I want the children to feel free to approach me. There is silence in the darkness for a moment and then I heard a small voice say, "Okay, Missionary, I'm coming."

Once the meal is finished and the dishes are cleared away, the villagers press into the little hut, filling it to capacity. One day, more than sixty people gather to hear the good news. Once everyone had found a place to sit, we sing a few songs and then, lit by the warm glow of a kerosene lantern, I teach God's Word, answer questions, pray for the sick, and lead those who wanted to follow Christ in a sinner's prayer. By the end of the week, there are ten who asked to be baptized in water. Today is my last morning in Itapu and the last chance for water baptism before I leave.

Leaving the small crowd of new believers on the beach with one of our local pastors I wade out into the rolling surf. The first round arc of the sun peaks over the horizon, gilding the scattered clouds with gold and painting the early morning waves a burnt orange. I find my footing in waist-deep water and motion for the first candidate for baptism to come forward. I listen to their testimonies; with each one I am thrilled again to be a witness of God's redeeming work. There in the swirling tide, with the new day dawning, I baptize them one by one.

After the last candidate has been baptized, I make my way back to the sandy shore. As the sun breaks full over the eastern horizon, we join together for a time of prayer, and I ask God to keep these new souls by his grace. Clothes are soaked through, faces are wet and shining, and water beads and glistens in their hair. I don't know that I have ever seen a more beautiful sight.

As we return to the village, they begin to sing and praise God. This is why I am a missionary. My touchstone in missions has always been Isaiah 42:12, "Let them give glory unto the LORD, and declare his praise in the islands." (KJV) Our purpose is to know Christ and make him known. When people begin to praise God, it is because they too now know Christ.

People in Vanuatu speak more than 120 different languages, yet Revelation 5:9 declares that as we worship around the throne, we will say of Christ, you "redeemed us to God by thy blood out of every kindred, and tongue, and people, and nation." (KJV) In that day, someone from every language in Vanuatu will be worshiping Christ around his throne.

Several times now in the course of our ministry in Vanuatu, I have been privileged to hear new believers from a previously unreached village break into song praising their redeemer. When I hear such new Christians praising God in their own languages, I get goose bumps, for I know I am hearing a preview of heaven.

As we pass by the banyan tree where John Paton tied his boat when he first came ashore more than 150 years ago, they begin to sing in their village language. Heads back and eyes closed, they sing with all their might. I hope that God allowed John Paton a quick glimpse over the balconies of heaven to view the great grandchildren of the cannibals that he preached to so long ago as they declared his praise in the islands!

What Is a God?

Franklin had a four-foot idol in his home. He had carved it with great attention to detail after careful study of a series of photos of traditional idols from a museum in Paris. Franklin told me the name of the idol and explained quite a bit about his ancestors' worship of this particular deity. Collectors will pay significant sums for authentic Melanesian idols hand carved by Ni-Vanuatu if they precisely match those from the pre-Christian era. But Franklin was a professing Christian who seemed quite serious about his faith, so I asked him how he reconciled his carving idols with the second commandment, "Thou shalt not make unto thee any graven image."

"Oh" he scoffed, "they're not gods."

Many villages in Vanuatu have a carving at each entrance of the village crafted from giant tree ferns known locally as black palms. The wood of the black palm is midnight black and has the texture of thick, matted, course hair. These carvings are often referred to as "guardians." They tend to consist of massively oversized heads with enormous eyes and male genitalia. The texture of the black fern makes it easy for other smaller ferns to take root on the carvings, making them seem to grow hair.

Every Ni-Vanuatu I ever asked about these guardians insisted that they were not gods but merely decorations. I almost believed them until a man on a nearby island defaced one of what the chief then referred to as the "sacred" guardians, prompting bloodshed."

Chief Jack didn't have any confusion about what a god is. "I am a god," he told me. I guess I must have looked skeptical because he proceeded to give me the evidence. "I go to my men's house. I drink a shell of kava. I proclaim, 'My wife will have a son!' Then I spit on the ground. Nine months later my wife has a son. Or I say, 'My wife will have a daughter!' Then I spit on the ground. Nine months later my wife has a daughter." He smiled. "You see, I am a god because I speak and there is life; my wife is a goddess because she gives birth to life."

I smiled at Chief Jack's comments. How to answer him? So I asked, "Will you do a favor for me? Will you put another star in the sky?" The chief dropped his head. There is an enormous difference between the power of men and the power of God. I am not sure about the chief's ability to predict the gender of his next child—he seemed pretty confident—but I know a few things about God.

God spoke, and the sun, moon, and stars sprang into existence. At his command, the waters of the sea parted and dry ground appeared. With the Word of his mouth, life in every form sprang forth on the earth. He handcrafted a man from the dust of the earth and bent down from the heights of heaven to blow breath into him and he became a living soul.

In Psalm 19:1 David said, "The heavens declare the glory of God; and the firmament sheweth his handywork. Day unto day uttereth speech, and night unto night sheweth knowledge. There is no speech nor language, where their voice is not heard." (KJV)

After my conversation with Chief Jack, I stood on the rim of Mount Yasur. The sun was going down in the west as the moon rose in the east. The coastline of Tanna stretched out before me like a silver thread on a black cloth as the moonlight reflected off the breakers. The sulfur-heavy smoke rolled out of the gaping crater, permeating the air with its scent. Hot gases rushed out of tears in the ground, filling the night with a perpetual roar.

As I drank in the wonder of the scene before me, I felt the ground tremble beneath my feet. The sound of an enormous explosion forcefully hit my chest, and a geyser of glowing red lava erupted a little more than a thousand feet in front of me, soaring hundreds of feet into the air before crashing back down to line the walls of the crater. That evening, Mount Yasur erupted a dozen times for us, giving off a dazzling display of fireworks under a starlit sky. I was entranced by the beauty of the scene, awed by the power of the eruptions.

There on the cusp of the volcano, I heard not a god, but the God speaking. No, his voice was not in the roar of hot gases escaping the vent or in the echoing thunder of the eruptions. His voice spoke silently from the stars, the moon, and the outline of mountains that form the island of Tanna. His works bore witness to his existence and even his nature.

He sent me here not to proclaim his existence—he already loudly proclaimed that. He sent me here to proclaim his mercy in the person of his Son.

Who is like our God?

Pax Americana

On the islands of Tanna and Santo, the name "America" is said with a special reverence. There is a cultural memory of World War II and the American soldiers that protected Vanuatu. Hundreds of thousands of American soldiers washed over these islands like a tsunami on their way to the bloody battlefields of Guadalcanal. Their technological superiority amazed the Ni-Vanuatu, their seemingly endless wealth staggered them, the relative equality between white and black soldiers stunned them, and the kindness shown by our fighting men enamored them to America forever. Many times I have been given the best chair and served the best food, not because I am a missionary, but because I am "Man America."

The signs of this American tsunami are everywhere in Vanuatu. From my front porch, I can see the graveyard of the USS *Calvin Coolidge*, a luxury liner converted into a troop carrier that was then lost to an American mine. The town of Luganville was a swamp until American Seabees drained it, built a sea wall, and filled it with earth. Our roads, including the one that runs in front of my house and the ones at the Bible Training Center, are just one example of many vital pieces of infrastructure built by American servicemen. Amazingly, these roads are still usable sixty-five years later in spite of precious little maintenance. While building our house, we found numerous unexploded shells from the war. In fact, we still find them occasionally with the lawn mower, a very disturbing and potentially explosive experience!

What many Americans do not recognize is that the effect of that tsunami of American military might has marked our entire world, a mark sometimes referred to as the "Pax Americana," Latin for "The Peace of America." A free and strong United States of America ushered in peace unprecedented in history. While this may seem a strange observation in a time of war, it is in fact true, especially when we discuss the period between World War II and the present. Not that there has been an absence of conflict, but that conflagrations that in previous eras engulfed continents or even the entire globe are quickly slipping out of living memory. They are relegated instead to black-and-white photos in stately museums or gory Hollywood renditions of dubious historical accuracy.

Living abroad has taught me that American power, while intended to preserve the liberties of Americans, in fact preserves the liberties of billions outside our borders. Many nations, like Vanuatu, spend virtually nothing on defense. Instead, their limited governments are able to focus on vital services like education, health care, and infrastructure. What protects a small defenseless nation like Vanuatu from domination by opportunistic foreign powers? Pax Americana. Rogue nations curtail their foreign adventures out of fear of American intervention.

This might seem an unfair burden on the American taxpayer. However, Pax Americana, preserved by our overwhelming military might, has repeatedly held the world back from the chaos of war. It has allowed global trade, travel, communication, and scientific collaboration to continue virtually unhindered, creating explosive growth in modern technologies, which, in turn, have yielded an unprecedented rise in the American and global standards of living.

Some have suggested that this period of relative tranquility has come to an end, that our crushing debt, faltering economy, porous borders, and lack of political will mean that America will soon fade from the global scene. The truth is that what we do as a nation—the leaders we elect, the laws they enact, and so on—do matter. They have worldwide consequences.

Like millions of Americans, I celebrated our independence on the Fourth of July. It was a time of great food, fellowship, and games with friends and our adopted family. Across our nation and around the world, wherever Americans gathered, stories were told, laughter shared, too much food was eaten, and aging men showed themselves to be woefully inadequate at games like baseball, football, and volleyball. Hopefully, there was time for thankfulness for a free nation and remembrance for those who gave so much that we might live free. From the first citizen soldiers who bled at Lexington to the young men and women fighting around the world today, a tragic price has been and is being paid for our liberty.

Today as I write, a team from the Joint POW/MIA Accounting Command is busy in the jungles of Santo. Their mission is to retrieve the remains of aircraft crews that were lost here during World War II. Local legends tell of pilots that pressed the attack in support of the marines holding Henderson Field beyond the point of their fuel limits, sacrificing their ability to reach their base to support their comrades in arms on the field.

In a few weeks, flag-draped coffins will again be leaving Pekoa Airport, over sixty years after these airmen fell. They will be returned to a nation that I trust has not forgotten their sacrifice.

Nanny in the Outhouse

The thud of a rat dropping from the rafters above my head wakes me up. I never like waking up in the middle of the night, but waking up when it is pouring rain and the only toilet is fifty yards away is significantly worse. I mumble bad things about rats in the night and grope for my flashlight. I fight my way clear of my mosquito net, slip on my sandals, and stumble over and around sleeping pastors. I pause at the door, bemoaning the pouring rain, and try to convince myself that this trip to the outhouse really is necessary.

Outhouses are a consistent challenge here in Vanuatu. Sometimes they are a source of trauma and tears, and other times of drama and laughter. I have discovered that there are several styles of outhouse. They range from "go feed the pigs," which is a fork in a tree surrounded by thick brush, to "VIP," which features a roof, four walls, and an actual toilet complete with a seat that, with the aid of a bucket of water, flushes all your troubles away.

Several other styles fall between these extremes. There is your split-log outhouse that consists of two small posts stretched over an open pit. Good balance, relatively recent construction, and shoes that can grip wet surfaces are the keys to using these without incident. Then there is your basic squatty potty that consists of a wooden or cement floor with a rugged hole in the middle. Yet another version is the hollow-log potty (I have pictures), where a length of hollow log is wedged in place over the waiting pit. Concrete thrones are common; nearly always too tall, they can be the most challenging type.

Toilet seats are a rare luxury. For squatty potties, this is not an issue. However, with rough concrete or splinter-inducing wooden thrones, this can be discouraging for the uninitiated. In my premission days, I was leery of public toilets in America, often fashioning impromptu toilet seat covers with tissue. That person would be shocked at the toilets I sit on these days. I have even developed a toilet mantra. I mutter, "Oh, Lord, sanctify this toilet," before I get down to business.

I have many memories of outhouses, none of them pleasant. Watching hundreds of roaches swarm up out of the pit in response to the light from a kerosene lantern on Ha'afava convinced me to never shine any form of light during my night visits and has made me a bit skittish about crawling sensations in the nether regions. An encounter with a six-inch centipede in a church outhouse on Achin had made me nervous about things brushing my feet in the dark. And while outhouses are always pungent, a wooden box-style privy on Mota Lava that was infested with fire ants made for my most poignant outhouse memory.

Outhouses in Vanuatu occasionally do not have walls, often are lacking roofs, rarely have doors, and never have toilet paper. If "go feed the pigs" is rated as a 1 and a "VIP" toilet is a 10, then the outhouse I am headed for tonight rates a 7. It boasts a thatch roof, woven palm frond walls, a curtain door, and a wooden throne of practical height with only a few splinters in waiting. The hole is freshly dug; thus, the air inside is only mildly aromatic.

I pat my pocket to confirm that I am carrying toilet paper, duck my head, and splash my way through the rain to the rustic latrine. I flash my light inside briefly to ensure that it is unoccupied before darting in, careful to extinguish my flashlight before it coaxes any roaches out of their hiding places. I transfer my flashlight to my mouth and gingerly feel my way to the throne, whispering my mantra as I go. Wary of centipedes, I take the paper out of my pocket and place it close to my feet.

Sure that all is in order, I settle on to the throne to take care of my business. Once seated, I become aware of a heady odor that is distinctly nonhuman. *What the...?* I wonder.

Suddenly I freeze, and the hair on the back of my neck rises. Something with coarse hair rubs my exposed thigh. I quickly forget my no-light-in-the-outhouse rule and shine the light on my companion. "Baaa," says the goat as it munches on one of the wall's palm fronds. She then squats and lets loose a stream of urine that inundates the floor. "Nice," I mutter.

It rained for the entire week I spent in that village. The goat moved into the outhouse to escape the downpour and slowly ate away the walls, providing commentary and companionship all week long.

Never Mind the Waves, Watch the Tide

I am holding the hand of a smiling old lady. She is a large woman, though her bulk is concealed well by an enormous Mother Hubbard dress. Her hair is grey. Her face is well lined with age. Laugh lines radiate from her surprisingly clear eyes. Her broad smile reveals only one tooth. As we talk, I realize that her mind is clear and that her hearing is unimpaired. Her back is straight, and her handshake is firm. She rises from her chair to greet me with relative ease. If I were to guess her age, I would say she is in her late sixties. She tells me she is 101 years old.

Ni-Vanuatu tend to age quickly. Retirement for those who hold government jobs is at fifty. A lack of dental care, primitive or nonexistent medical care, malaria, and an overall hard life give both men and women a relatively short life span. The average life expectancy of women is lower than that of men because so many of them die in childbirth, making this lady an incredible exception.

I tend to be skeptical of claims of old age in Vanuatu. Few Ni-Vanuatu know their birth dates, either the day or the year. I once had a gentleman tell me that he was at least ninety. When I asked him if he was already married when the Americans arrived in 1944, he replied, "Of course not.

I wasn't born yet." Many Ni-Vanuatu look ancient when, in fact, they wouldn't qualify for retirement in the United States.

I have known this old lady for the last eight years and have never heard anyone refer to her by anything other than Olfala Mama, or "The Old Mother." She is the mother of John Tari, a prominent chief and landowner on Santo. She is the matriarch of Shalom Assembly of God in Nambualou— the second Pentecostal church established on Santo.

Since I am skeptical of the claim that she is a centenarian, I ask her if she remembers the Americans coming. "Oh my, yes," she replies. "I was the age of my granddaughter there." She points to a woman in her early thirties surrounded by her children.

I was impressed but still not convinced. "What year were you born?" I ask.

She laughs. "I don't have any idea when I was born. I started counting my age when I married. I assume that I was nearly eighteen when I married, and I was married eighty-three years ago."

My mind reels when I try to comprehend the changes that have happened during her life. In 1926, the year that she married, Santo was still a wild and savage place. There were no roads, virtually no contact with the outside world. Headhunters still ruled a majority of the island; in fact, twenty years after her marriage, they would bring the shrunken heads of their captured enemies down to the brothels to sell as souvenirs to American soldiers.

When this lady started her life, the gospel had not gone beyond the seashore. French and English governments bickered over who was in control, and the island had parallel French and British governments, judicial systems, police forces, jails, and post offices. Cars, telephones, electricity, and airplanes were unknown. The only schools were in scattered missions, and few children attended.

She was on hand to watch as the American military swept in like a wave, bringing over five hundred thousand troops, including famous units like the Black Sheep Squadron and famous people like Douglas MacArthur, James Michener, and Eleanor Roosevelt. Overnight, a town was born, roads were pushed through what had been deemed impenetrable jungle, and airports were carved out of hilltops. Trucks, radios, movies, peanut butter, Coca-Cola, and ice cream are just a few of the things that the Americans introduced to the Ni-Vanuatu.

She was there to watch when the wave of troops rolled out again, and all those young men were gone, their jeeps, trucks, and bulldozers pushed off into the ocean. How quiet and still it must have seemed. She watched as the town they built rusted away and the jungle reclaimed their roads and airports.

In her lifetime, the gospel has spread to nearly every corner of Santo. Headhunting has become a thing of the past. She grew up with children who would be the victims of headhunters, and now she watches her great-grandchildren playing in the churchyard, the young ones playing with cheap Chinese-made toys, the older ones texting their friends on mobile phones.

In missions it is easy to get too focused on the present. I find myself getting discouraged over a pastor who backslides or a promising Bible school student who has a moral failure. I get frustrated by the superstition that persists among Christians and the syncretism, or mixing of old and new religious ideas into a hodgepodge, that is questionably Christian. I chafe at what seem to be endless delays in getting churches built and pastors trained and in reaching the remaining unreached tribes and villages in Vanuatu.

What a difference a hundred years of perspective makes. The transformation that the gospel makes in a country may seem to be slow, but it is unceasing and unrelenting. Slowly but consistently, what seems unchangeable is changed. It is not a wave that sweeps in and then out again, leaving only a few rusted relics as evidence of its passing. No, it is a mighty tide that builds and builds and cannot be resisted.

If one hundred years of perspective makes such a change, what must be the view from God's eyes? How easy it is to get caught up in a narrow focus on numbers of adherents or buildings that have been built. Goals that we set for this year or this term seem to be vitally important, but God promises to reward faithfulness, not accomplishments. I am reminded how B. H. Clendenin liked to quote William Booth's words of wisdom to his daughter: "Never mind the waves; keep your eyes on the tide."

The Hunter

The man crouched at the edge of the jungle, the ferns and leafy plants obscuring his form. His skin was a deep brown. His frame, wiry and muscled, was uncovered; only his penis was clothed in a wrapping called a *numbas*. His hair, coal black and beaded with the early morning dew, was formed into long natural dreadlocks, flat on top of his head and spread out in a great circle like a primeval halo to the sides. His arms held a battered rifle. His eyes were shining, intense, the eyes of a hunter. His nostrils were stuffed with leaves blessed by the village shaman. As he waited in silence, very subtly, his right nostril began to twitch. The leaf seemed to be vibrating, humming. It was telling him, singing to him, "Today you will be successful in the hunt."

The movement caught his eye: another man, slow, cautious, wary of unseen danger, paused under the towering banyan tree that shaded the *nasara*, or dancing ground. The hunter froze as the second man gazed at the surrounding jungle, his eyes sliding over the familiar foliage. Nothing was amiss. He relaxed and stretched to work out the early morning kinks in his muscles.

Slowly the hunter lifted the rifle to his shoulder. His eyes peered down the rusty iron sights. His trigger finger squeezed. The rifle leaped backward, crashing into his shoulder, the sound splitting the silence of the morning. The second man's face exploded, teeth and bits of bone flying across the clearing as he fell to the earth. The hunter's face beamed with a huge smile. His eyes danced as he contemplated the feast that awaited him.

His eyes are still dancing. Today I am sitting across from the hunter. He is no longer a strong warrior. His skin is still dark, but his hair is now snow white. His muscles are slack—he can walk only with the help of a cane. Yet his eyes still dance. He has just mimed for me the story of his triumphant hunt. His face is a mass of wrinkles as he cackles, remembering his victim's face exploding.

The question is asked first in English, and it takes a long trip before it reaches the old man. First it is translated to Bislama, then to the language of the Big Numbas, and finally to sign language. The hunter is stone deaf. "Did you eat him?" I watch his reaction. His smile flees and his face crumples, those dancing eyes, now filled with shame and guilt, begin to tear. "No, no, no!" The answer grows more emphatic each time he says it, his horror with the idea growing. The monstrosity of it surely fills his mind. Now his memories haunt him; remorse floods him.

Yet the hunter is here today for one reason: I have asked to interview those who practiced cannibalism. In fact he has bragged to his family many times that he ate not only this victim but many others. His contemporaries all attest, "He was a mighty warrior. He killed and ate many." I understand his denial. Were I guilty, I too would deny it. His response is classic of those cannibals who have never come to know Christ. They feel so much shame, guilt, and remorse, yet they have no way to expunge the record and redeem themselves.

I long to tell him that there is one who paid the price. He carried your guilt. He paid the price for your peace. But my words would fall on deaf ears, stone deaf ears. This hunter needs to hear the gospel so desperately, but I have come too late. A few years earlier he could have heard and believed. Today it is too late; the twilight of his life darkens.

Why do I go into the bush? Why do I climb mountains, eat unmentionable foods, and sleep on dirt floors in Stone Age villages? Because there are other hunters out there. Men who need to hear, who need to know. For them it is not too late, not yet.

So while it is day, I must work. For night cometh, when no man can work.

Pizza with the President

I make my way to the table in the middle of the schoolroom, and pick up a second piece of pizza. I have just taken my first bite when I notice the speaker of parliament, currently the acting president of Vanuatu while the president is incapacitated by a medical issue. He motions for me to join him. I swallow quickly and walk over to him. We talk about my sermon, my future in Vanuatu, and past meals we have shared. As we talk, my mind races, trying to figure out what to do with the piece of pizza in my hand. Do I eat it or let it get cold? I have a request for him; do I dare share it? Just how bold can you be when talking to the president of your host country? "Your Excellency, there is one thing I would like to discuss with you," I hear myself saying, amazed at my own audacity. Nothing like divine appointments...

At a state dinner the night before, the acting president leaned over to whisper to the pastor sitting next to him, "Pastor, I am tired of all the formalities and ceremonies. Tomorrow I am coming to your church. I want to come not as the president but as a worshiper. Do me a favor; keep the formalities to a minimum."

The dinner ended around nine o'clock, and by then Pastor Dick was in full panic mode; an honor guard of Royal Rangers must be prepared, the Missionettes needed to make leis, the church needed to be double checked and then cleaned again, fresh flowers were needed, and a special speaker must be found. Who to ask on such short notice? Who else? The missionary.

My phone rang at half past nine. "Sorry to disturb you, Missionary, but I need to ask a favor." There was no question in his mind or mine what my answer would be; at that point I owed Pastor Dick so many favors that the answer had to be yes. "Missionary, the acting president of Vanuatu and his delegation will be visiting Calvary Temple tomorrow. Do you think you could prepare a short sermon that would be appropriate?"

My mind went back to a verse Robert Holmes liked to quote to a group of prospective missionaries at Bible school, Proverbs 22:29: "Seest thou a man diligent in his business? he shall stand before kings; he shall not stand before mean men." (KJV) Since then I have had audiences with kings, prime ministers, and presidents.

One Sunday when I was speaking in the Kingdom of Tonga, my interpreter was really struggling to keep up, and an elderly man in the audience interrupted to ask if I would mind if he interpreted. He finished the sermon in fantastic style. It was only after the service that I learned he was the prime minister and brother to the king!

It is funny the way things look different when you're sitting in front of a head of state.

Just the day before, I had given away my new Bislama Bible. My old one had lost the binding and was literally falling apart. I'd had it for nine years and preached thousands of sermons out if it. It followed me around to some seventy islands, into the shadow of five different volcanoes, across untamed rivers, and over too many mountains to count. It always seemed good enough before, but this morning it looked tattered and pitiful. I found myself wishing that I had a sleek leather-bound Bible with a matching portfolio. Instead, I had my worn-out Bible and a bright red and white notebook.

I also felt self-conscious about my clothes. The slacks I was wearing had a tear at the pocket. I adjusted the borrowed suit coat to cover the blemish, but my shoe smiled a gaping toothless grin up at me from where the sole was separating at the ball of the foot. I saw remnants of the glue from my last repair. *Lord, help the service to hurry up so that I can hide behind the pulpit.* We try to make our clothes stretch for the length of each four year term we live in Vanuatu; ten months out from our return to the States, things were starting to get a bit threadbare. They seemed good enough most of the time, but this morning I sure wished I had something better.

I felt better once I was in the pulpit. I had learned the protocol for addressing government dignitaries here in Vanuatu, and I smoothly slid through the proper acknowledgments. I took my text from John 8 and preached about finding spiritual freedom. Before the pulpit, all men are equal.

After service we were invited to have pizza with the pastor and government dignitaries. There, standing in the schoolroom at Santo Christian School, I had the opportunity to present my case to the acting president. I never cease to be amazed at how God arranges accidental audiences just when we need them most.

I remembered when I had made an error on a customs declaration for a container of building supplies a few years before. Appeals to the customs department seemed to fall on deaf ears, and other missionaries were filling my mind with horror stories of their donated goods being seized and auctioned off when they failed to make proper declarations. The error was mine, and I expected no relief. One afternoon some time later, a local pastor realized he had inadvertently booked two weddings for the same day and asked me to fill in for him at the one in town. I stood beside the groom at the altar and watched in amazement as none other than the customs director walked the lovely bride down the aisle. At the reception, I mentally debated the propriety of bringing the matter to his attention. As I struggled with my conscience and the local cultural mores, he approached me. "Missionary, bring a letter by my office and I will see to it your supplies are released."

Maybe today had been arranged for just such a purpose. "Your Excellency, there is one thing I would like to discuss with you. We have a young missionary couple here that seems to be having a difficult time getting a visa."

"Missionary," the acting president says, "just bring a letter by my office."

Hidden in the Rain

Glittering black volcanic ash, massive spreading banyan trees. Brilliantly colored grass skirts sway; the rain forest reverberates with rhythmic chants. A ring of dancers springs into the air, coiling their legs and collectively slamming wide bare feet into the nasara. The ground trembles, crashing rain falls like a blanket across the valley, cutting off the outside world, the rest of the island, and finally the rest of the valley, until only this is left. This is holy ground in Tanna; they call it Imrawang.

This is the scene that Brandon Forester and I came upon during our recent ministry survey to the Enmantange valley in South Tanna. It was Sunday afternoon, and we had finished with a service in the village of Nazareth, one of only two Assembly of God enclaves in the entire valley, and were headed to visit a nearby village. Our purpose in coming was to visit each village in the valley, gathering information on population, their religious beliefs, the leadership structure of the local chiefs, their language and tribal boundaries, and their access to things like medical facilities, schools, and clean water. The idea was not so much to engage in ministry but to gather knowledge, to know the conditions and needs of the area in order to develop an effective ministry strategy.

Each village heralded our arrival in the same way—bony village dogs barked the alarm, tucking their tails between their legs and slowly retreating before us; round-eyed naked children clung to their mothers' skirts and peeked out at us from low-slung, smoke-filled thatch houses; intensely shy but curious women and girls that seemed to be mere children balanced babies on their hips and clustered in chattering groups at doorways and around firepits. Our guide provides respectful introductions to the local chief, and we are issued a formal invitation to talk in the *nakamal* or meeting ground.

After prolonged introductions, I ask my questions. "What is the name of this place?," "What is your religion?", and on and on.

Then it is time for their questions. "Why have you come?" This is my favorite question. It gives me my opening, and starting with Creation and the Fall, I weave my story in Bislama. I assume nothing, and slowly and patiently, I tell the story of the Creator God who by virtue of his ownership dictated a moral code in our hearts. Deliberately using the moral code of the local kustom religion, I make the case that starting with Adam, all people have sinned and are guilty before God. Starting in the Garden and following with the teachings of James and Romans, I outline the consequences of our actions.

Finally in John chapters three and one I explore the remedy: even though sin has produced death in us, there is hope; God has provided us a means of new life. Decisions for Christ during these initial presentations of the gospel are rare. There is just too much information to assimilate at once. Too many new concepts at once. But a seed is planted, one that others can water and the Holy Spirit can cultivate.

What are the results of our efforts? We discover that there are twenty-two villages with an average population of just over one hundred, nearly twice as many as we had been told. The valley is not quite as unreached as we were led to believe. In addition to the two Assembly of God outstations, there is also a small Catholic mission and a Presbyterian church with several of its own outstations in surrounding villages. We find that the villages in the center of the valley have been evangelized but that villages on both ends remain unreached.

As we near the end of our trek Brandon and I were making our way up a narrow path, thick brush crowding on each side with massive trees arching over us, when we became aware of chants and a faint trembling in the ground. As we rounded the corner, our path opened into an enormous round nasara of sparkling black ash, framed by colossal banyan trees whose thick tangle of branches, roots, and vines formed awe-inspiring living walls.

Centered on the nasara was a ring of women and girls dressed in thick, multicolored grass skirts surrounding a ring of men. At the very center danced a naked baby boy of two. Their chants flooded the air and their feet thudded into the ground in unison, making even the mighty banyans tremble. The rings span leaped high in the air and crashed down into the black earth. The rain ran to join them; racing over the mountains and thundering across the floor of the valley, it slammed into us.

Rivulets sprang to life across the floor of the nasara, wet bodies glistened, dew beads formed on bouncing hair, and feet splattered puddles as the rain and the rings danced together. In the middle, the small boy danced, rain gathering in his hair and streaming down his face. For a second, his round eyes caught and held mine, and I wondered as to the meaning of this dance.

A few minutes later, our guide appeared out of the rain and led us around the dancers and beyond the nasara. As the noise of the chants faded behind the din of the rain, I asked him repeatedly to tell me the meaning of the dance, to translate the chants, but he refused; the meaning remains hidden in the rain.

Salt and Light

I am standing beside the rim of a volcanic crater. The ground is composed of dark gray volcanic ash and devoid of any vegetation. The ground shakes, and a muffled boom reverberates through the trees. No, it's not this crater erupting; they tell me this one is extinct. The live one, however, is less than five miles away. Knowing that, I am not confident about how extinct this one is.

This is the village of Itapu, or "Holy Place." It is holy because it is believed to be the birthplace of the volcano, Mount Yasur. The houses of the village are built literally on the edge of the crater. I am here because of a chance meeting on the path. I am here to pick out the building spot for a new church.

While making my way through the Enmantange valley in preparation for the arrival of a team from Health Care Ministries, I met Chief Jack on the path. He and his men were coming from the jungle on the mountainside above us when our guide saw them. "Wait, Missionary," he told me. "This could be a really good opportunity; this man is a prominent chief."

I waited and spoke with Chief Jack; after a few minutes of conversation with me and rest for his men, he announced that I would be coming to his village the next day. I started to hedge since I didn't know where his village was and how it would fit into our plans, but my guide quickly cut me off and said we would be happy to be there the following day.

When I first walked into Itapu, I had no idea that it was on the rim of a volcanic crater. I was hot, tired, and thirsty. My guide brought me to an opening in the middle of the village and offered me a low stool. The men of the village gathered in front of me while a group of women sat by themselves off to the side. We exchanged a few words of introduction, and then Chief Jack asked me to tell them why I had come to their island.

I planted my walking stick in the ground and started with Creation; for the next hour, I wove in the story of God's plan of redemption. I ended with Jesus's conversation with Nicodemus in John 3. When I finished, the men began to question me. I knew from the looks on their faces that these would not be friendly questions.

One questioner was particularly hostile. "I meet a lot of tourists from America," he told me. "They tell me about war, murder, drugs, and people without homes who have to sleep on the streets. They tell me that in America, you must lock your home at night or thieves will steal even your children. If your religion didn't work in America, why are you bringing it to us?"

On the surface, it looked like a good question. Has Christianity failed in America? If it has, then why export it? But in truth, this question revealed several assumptions—that religion is basically a system of rules, that a nation would have only one religion, and that the system of rules imposed by that one religion would become the de facto laws of that nation, thereby governing the behavior of everyone.

The truth is that Christianity is not about religion. It is about relationship: each man, woman, boy, or girl experiencing the life of God. Christianity is salt and light in a culture: it does transform it, but it does not force conformity to its teachings.

People can choose evil, and some do. A nation can know the truth about Christ and the life available in him and still choose to reject him. This is what Paul was talking about in Romans 1:18, "The wrath of God is being revealed from heaven against all the godlessness and wickedness of men who suppress the truth by their wickedness" (NIV). Men who know the truth yet choose to live wickedly are actively suppressing the truth. This is why despite three hundred years of Christianity in America, there is the tragedy of a culture rotting away from moral decay.

I have not come to Vanuatu to change the religion or culture to mirror America. The goal of missions is not to create mini Americas or utopian societies, but to present individuals with the opportunity to find peace with God and eternal life. I have come to introduce Jesus Christ to those who do not know him. Each individual in the village of Itapu faced a decision of what to do with Christ. Those who would choose to believe in him would have the right to become the sons of God and to experience an incredible transformation in their lives.

I silently prayed for wisdom before answering my questioner. Carefully, I tried to point out the difference between relationship and religion. I explained that I was not trying to force my religion on his village or on Vanuatu. Instead, I was coming with the good news that all men can have peace with God and share in his life.

I can't say I won over that particular questioner that day; however, enough people chose Christ to form the nucleus of a church. Today, construction is underway on the Itapu Assembly of God church. Now it is up to them to be the salt and light.

Pierre

The ship is gently bobbing at anchor just off of Craig's Cove on the island of Ambrym. The night air is filled with the deep throbbing rumble of the diesel engines below deck and the high-pitched whines of small outboard engines. Search lights mounted on the super structure of the ship illuminate the small beach landing and the trail of small boats ferrying passengers and freight to the shore. In the glow of the searchlights, volcanic ash floats gently down around us, like a caustic snow. I have come to Craig's Cove, pronounced as a very guttural "cray cough," by the locals because of a most unusual man, Pierre.

Pierre looks like a rough man, not a bad man, though he was that before, but a rough man. Before coming to Christ, Pierre worked on a Taiwanese fishing boat. One day in a fit of rage, he murdered a significant portion of the crew, giving him the distinction of being one of a very few mass murderers in recent times in Vanuatu. On one hand, this makes the average person slightly nervous around Pierre; on the other hand, he is somewhat famous. The fact that his victims were foreigners makes his crimes a little more palatable to the average Ni-Vanuatu, so that many years after he completed his prison sentence and committed his life to Christ, he remains to some extent feared, yet notorious in a not all together negative way.

A year before, Pierre had enrolled as a student at Sanma Bible Training Center. Over that year, we poured over God's Word together, prayed together, and conducted countless evangelistic outreaches and children's Bible clubs together. Together we climbed mountains, forded rivers, slogged through swamps, slept on dirt floors of thatch huts scattered through the jungle, and planted churches in the unreached villages of his fellow students. Now it is Pierre's turn. Ambrym is his island, Craig's Cove is his village, and we have come together once more to plant a church.

If Pierre is rough, Craig's Cove is hard. That night as we wait to disembark the ship, I develop an impression of Craig's Cove that strengthens over time; the impressions that this is going to be a difficult place. The landing is stony, so much so that the ship cannot approach the shore but anchors a quarter mile off shore. Banana boats ferry us to the beach. Stepping out barefoot onto the beach, I find it consists more of broken bits of coral and sharp lava than sand. Using the search lights from the ship, we put on boots, headlamps, and backpacks and prepare in the inky darkness to portage our supplies over the rocky trail from the landing to the village.

Craig's Cove is not just hard physically, but spiritually as well. Ambrym, home to one of Vanuatu's active volcanoes, is steeped in witchcraft. Ni-Vanuatu almost always perceive volcanoes as being reservoirs of spiritual power. Thus, Ambrym hosts sacred fire, three-headed tomtoms, the Rom dances, and even hints of human sacrifice. At Craig's Cove, Catholicism has been added to this mix of wizardry and secret societies. This is indeed stony ground.

All together, our outreach to Craig's Cove extends over two months. There is precrusade evangelism of door-to-door soul winning and literature distribution, a free clinic and medicine, children and youth ministries, daily Bible classes for new converts, and two weeks of crusade services. Opposition came from all sides—Catholic leaders threaten their members with discipline if they attend, chiefs place a taboo on any locals participating, and leaders of secret societies scoff at the power of a white man's god. My impression that this is a hard place is proved daily by low attendance at the meetings and many "Nicodemus" conversions— people who want to find the blessings of peace with God but are not willing to bear the persecution that would follow a public confession of Christ.

The Sunday before our departure, we lead a handful of new believers to the shore for water baptism; unlike other villages where we have planted churches, there is no solid core for the pastor to start with, there are no elders to appointment, and no church government to set in place. Instead there is Pierre, his wife and children, and a handful of young people brave enough to join the new church. As we prepare to leave Ambrym, I knew we are leaving behind a very discouraged Pierre. From the look on the faces of Pierre and his wife that Sunday I wonder if he and his family wouldn't be joining us on the return trip.

Over the next three years, I receive mixed reports from Craig's Cove, one would tell me that Pierre was being faithful, that the church was still there, and others would report that what group had existed had disbanded and that Pierre was no longer trying to establish the church. The area we serve is so vast and travel so costly and difficult in Vanuatu that I had not been able to return to Craig's Cove myself; yet I continued to pray for Pierre and that small group we had left behind on that stony beach.

Last week I received a call from Pastor Dick, our presbyter, "Missionary, you need to come to my house, there is someone here you would like to see." On arriving at Pastor Dick's house, I was met by Pierre. After the usual exchange of greetings required in Vanuatu, I said, "Tell me, Pierre, how is the church?"

Over the next hour, Pastor Dick, Pastor Simon, and I listened to the story of the church at Craig's Cove; a story of trial and difficulty. "Missionary, in the months after you left everyone abandoned us. For two years it was just my family and I." Then he began to tell us of the victories of the past year. It started with a widow woman who joined them; one by one he began to relate stories of men and women finding Christ. These stories in turn broadened into stories of surrounding villages that have opened to the gospel where he has established outstations.

Today a strong and vital church has taken root in the stony ground at Craig's Cove; it has no name, its building is little more than a thatch lean-to, but it is led by a determined local leader, is supported by local believers, and is reproducing itself in the surrounding communities.

This is what success in missions looks like.

Left Behind

Saying good-bye is never easy. We were standing in the departure lounge of the Santo Airport. Our plane had commenced boarding, and it was time to go. I watched as my daughter's friend clung to her. Big round tears welled up in her rich brown eyes and cascaded down her cheeks. I knew she would miss Alecia, but I also knew that she was grieving over more than just our leaving. This young lady had been the primary ministry partner and informally adopted daughter of another missionary couple. They had been forced to leave suddenly. For months we had been her last American friends on the island. Today she would be left behind, alone. There was much more going on here than what was visible on the surface.

Even the best intentioned missionaries can never completely assimilate to their host cultures. While they may adopt the local language, style of clothing, and diet, there are many cultural mores that are too deeply engrained to ever lay aside. However, over the course of their adaptation to their host culture, they lose some things. Try as they might, they are never truly American again.

Many cultural values are unspoken. These attitudes and values are never articulated because they are never challenged at home. Abroad, they are forcefully challenged and often discarded because once out in the open, they turn out to be illogical. Missionaries and their families become "third cultural," not really belonging to their home or their host cultures.

While this may appear to be a novel concept, missionaries and mission organizations have long accepted this as an inevitable result of prolonged immersion in one's host culture.

Seminars and workshops abound for helping missionaries and their children readapt to their home culture; in fact, the mascot of the International Society of Missionary Kids is a chameleon. Missionaries and their families often have to change their stripes to blend into their current environment; however, internally they are never quite the same as those around them.

Less often discussed are the other citizens of this third culture. Missionaries create a third-culture zone around them. The national workers that most often interact with missionaries also adapt and change. For the sake of harmonious working relationships, they often learn the missionaries' language, develop a taste for their cultural foods, and lay aside many of their own cultural presuppositions that conflict with the missionaries' culture. In the process, they lose a bit of their own cultural identity. Their world is a hybrid of two cultures, and they become a cultural anomaly to their own families.

Once the missionaries leave, the third-culture zone disappears. There are no more care packages with American goodies, American novels to read, or American videos to watch. A cherished friend has been lost, but something else has been lost as well. Values and perspectives that were continually reinforced in their interaction with their missionary friends are now subject to scorn and ridicule by their own friends and family. They try to see things from the same perspective as their fellow countrymen, but they just cannot. Their eyes have been opened to a different world. They are like pieces of a plastic jigsaw puzzle that have been warped by heat. They will never quite fit again.

They have made very real sacrifices for the gospel. They have gone through a painful transition in adapting to their missionary coworkers, and they will never be the same again. In addition, often when missionary personnel are replaced, the new missionaries refuse to associate with those same individuals who had inhabited the previous missionary's third-culture zone. I have heard new missionaries scornfully dismiss those third-culture partners of previous missionaries as "the missionary's pet" or "spoiled imitation Americans" and then obliviously go about creating their own pets.

What can be done?

First, prospective missionaries can anticipate this phenomenon. Recognize that it is not just you and your family that are reformed by the stress of this cross-cultural interaction. Others' lives will be changed as well. We must never use people regardless of how noble our goals may be. Choose to respect those fellow laborers who will inhabit your third-culture zone. Respect those who have done so with previous missionaries. Recognize that their previous cultural transformation gives them a huge advantage in working with you. Dip your bucket deep into this well of talent before seeking to create new third-culture partners.

Second, invite those into your third-culture zone who are highly resilient. Single young men and women separated from their families will be the most deeply changed. Their lack of a solid cultural fabric and support system leaves them very vulnerable. When the missionary leaves, they often have their whole world cut out from under them. They become strangers in their homeland. When possible, choose to work with men and women who are married and firmly grounded in the local church and social scene. Yes, they will be slower to adapt to your perspectives, but you will develop a much healthier relationship, as you will be forced to accept the larger half of the cultural transition. Your third-culture world will look more like their culture than yours.

Last, respect the price your third-culture partners are paying. Once I was trying to convince my ministry team to take a course of action that was countercultural. All of us agreed that the plan was more biblically sound than the status quo, yet I sensed a great deal of resistance to actually implementing the arrangement. I took my dilemma to Jack Rudd, an older missionary for whom I have great respect. After I laid out my scenario, Jack smiled and said, "Never forget that in the back of their minds they are always thinking, 'One day this missionary is going to get on the plane and leave.' No matter how badly things may turn out, they never have that option."

Today I left my third-culture partners behind. I wept with them and will pray for them till we meet again.

Kotu

The ocean is still. It is one of those things that is hard to believe until you have seen it—on the whole of the wide expanse, there is not one wave, not even a ripple. It is like a glass of the deepest blue. The hot sun beats down unmercifully, as there is not even a breath of wind. Sweat drips down browning and burned faces under wide-brimmed hats. Most of the faces are expressionless—tired from the sea journey and unsure of what lies ahead.

Ahead of us rises a tall, rounded volcanic island cloaked in emerald green. The bow of our boat shatters the glassy calm of the sea into a thousand sparkling prisms, and the deep blue yields to an aquamarine, then to the lightest of blues. Myriad colorful fish dart among brilliantly painted corals while graceful sea turtles flee the sound of our approaching outboard. Finally, the sea surrenders to the dull brown of tidal flats. We are under the very brow of the island Kotu.

Somehow it seems ominous. Slowly, we circle the island looking for a place to anchor. The only sign of life is the piercing call of tropical birds. I begin to wonder if anyone lives here at all. Yet somewhere, shrouded by the jungle, lies a village of several hundred people. As we round the southern point, we are greeted by the sight of an old shipwreck; battered by the storms, rusted by the never-ending assault of saltwater, it leans heavily upon the broken rocks. The island seems to challenge us, "See what comes to those who dare to seek entrance here." Soon after we spot a small jetty, beyond that a tiny mud trail struggling up the hillside before disappearing into the dense foliage.

I will never forget that trail. Red Tongan clay soaked in the rain the night before refuses to yield any traction. Clusters of wide-eyed children watch from a safe distance while we work our way up to the village, struggling, slipping, and sweating with several hundred pounds of generator, petrol, and electrical equipment. Village dogs rush out to threaten the outsiders but slink back into the bushes with their tails between their legs at the sight of white people.

This will be the first time that many of those who call Kotu home will have seen electric lights or heard the power of a PA system. While most have seen white men before, few have seen a white family. Renee and the children prove to be an almost irresistible attraction. Soon all work in the village has ceased and runners have been sent to the bush to call home the men. This is too great an event for anyone to miss.

We only have a limited amount of time as our boats can only make the passage from Kotu to our base island of Ha'afeva at the right tide. Tua, the noble's spokesman from Ha'afeva, has accompanied us. Even as he petitions the noble for permission to hold an evangelistic service, the team is setting up equipment and the crowd is swelling. The team ministers in song and many give their testimony of what God has done in their lives. I step forward, Bible in hand. Again, silence is the rule of the day; this time it is broken only by the sound of our generator.

I begin to share a timeless message, "You must be born again." The band begins to play softly. Quietly I make the appeal, *"Ha'u ki Sisu,"* "Come to Jesus," and they come; first one, then another, here a young woman, there an old man, six in all starting a new life in Christ.

The sun is starting to set, and once again we are standing on the little jetty, only this time we are encircled by six new Christians. With pleading eyes, they beg us not to go. *"Nofo pe ki heni, ik'i koe alu. Koe alu a'pongpongi."* "Don't go, stay at least till morning." Extended boat rides are bad, being on sinking boats is scary, the lack of indoor plumbing is unpleasant, and rats having the free reign of your room at night is worse, but in all of island ministry, the very worst is floating off into the sunset while brand-new Christians stand waving, weeping on the shore. Even though our hearts say stay, we go.

The setting sun lays a golden pathway across a shimmering ocean. Sleek tuna, shining like machined steel, leap into the air after fleeing squid while screaming seabirds circle and dart overhead. The sights are arresting, yet I wonder about the harvest, why after thirty years of an Assemblies of God presence in Tonga, no one has taken the simple gospel to Kotu. My mind slips away from the scenery to mission services I sat through as a child.

I can hear the bass voice of the missionary, my childhood hero. "I can guarantee you a soul for every dollar." That's one promise I can never keep. The trip to Kotu involved more than fourteen hours of boat travel on four different boats. The combined expenses of boat fare, equipment costs, and food for a team of twenty-eight had more than exceeded a thousand dollars. Less than three hundred people live on Kotu. If success in missions is defined in numbers, I have failed.

Then I hear the voice of another missionary. He is trying to explain to hard-hearted religious leaders why he spends so much time with sinners. He tells a story of a shepherd who had one hundred sheep. Ninety-nine are safe in the fold, but one is lost. "What will the shepherd do?" he asks. "Won't he leave the ninety-nine and search for the one lost? And when he finds that one, oh, what rejoicing there will be!"

I smile. You see, the shepherd just found a few more lost sheep.

The Day God Spoke

High in the cloud-cloaked mountains above the Enmantange Valley, a small stream gathers itself before leaping 120 feet into the ravine below. Once at the floor of the ravine, it gurgles from one pool to another, laughing as it leaps over small waterfalls and slicing its way back and forth over the gravel floor of the ravine like a downhill slalom skier. To the east of the village of Isaaka, it takes a hard swing to the right and swirls against the moss-covered rock wall of the ravine. There, sandwiched between the hard stone and a gravel bench, it forms a long, shaded, waist-deep pool before spilling over the pebble dam and continuing its journey to the arid ash plains of Mount Yasur.

I am standing in this pool, slowly going numb from cold from the waist down because God spoke to a chief. One week before, the chief of the village above the waterfall had come to Isaaka because his daughter had a toothache. I was there with a team of medical volunteers from Health Care Ministries, one of whom was a dentist. As his daughter was being treated, he visited with two local pastors, and by the end of the day, he had invited them to come to his home.

Pastors Joni Lava and Jimmy made the trip to the chief's home that Sunday. They left at daybreak in order to complete the four-hour trip by midmorning, aware that the trip there and back would require more than eight hours of walking. When they arrived, they conducted a service with the chief and his family, patiently explaining the plan of salvation and encouraging the family to choose Christ over the animism that they had followed for generations. The chief spoke for the family when he respectfully thanked them for coming but said that for them the old ways were best.

The next morning at dawn we were stunned to see the chief sitting outside of the clinic area. His face was drawn and his eyes were red from crying; earnestly he asked Pastor Joni to pray for him. "Last night, after you left, your God spoke to me. I heard your God speaking, it was as if there was a radio in my room. He told me, 'You have waited long enough; it is time for you to make peace with me.'"

Again Pastor Joni explained the plan of salvation, and this time he led a willing chief in the sinner's prayer. "Saturday, we will be having a baptism. If you are serious about following Christ, you should come," Pastor Joni told him before the chief began the four-hour walk back home.

Now I stand in a cold stream with my back to the stone wall, and before a crowd of believers, I baptize the chief and his wife, but this is not the end of the story. Two weeks later, I receive a phone call from a Wycliffe missionary on Tanna. She and her husband are translating the Bible into the language of the chief. "I just wanted you to know that there has been an incredible change in our chief," she told me. "He hasn't touched kava for the last two weeks!"

Kava is the local drug of choice, with the mass majority of men using it on a daily basis. In Tanna, kava is a nightly ritual. Before sunset, prepubescent boys chew the roots of the kava shrub to release the potent hypnotic found there. They spit out the chewed up roots into a kava bowl; water is then mixed with the masticated roots and spittle, making kava.

As the sun sets, the men of the village gather to drink the mixture. They squat around a nakamal, a clearing in the jungle surrounded by massive banyan trees, and in the gathering darkness use coconut shells to scoop multiple helpings out of the communal bowl. Their bodies and minds slowly go numb in the gathering gloom. Prior to coming to Christ, this is how the chief ended every day.

After he came to Christ, his daughter entered his home one evening to find her father sitting with a Bible open before him. She was surprised because she knew that her father was illiterate. "Dad, what are you doing?" she asked. "Can you read that?"

"No," he replied, "I just really want to know what it says." Through the ministry of the Wycliffe missionaries, audio portions of God's Word were made available to the chief. Now his evenings are different.

High in the cloud-cloaked mountains above the Enmantange valley, a small village nestles beside the stream. Just as it gathers itself to leap over the precipice, there, sitting in his smoke-filled thatch hut, an old chief slowly turns the hand crank on a portable tape player. What spills out is the voice of a man, but there in the haze an old chief hears God speaking to him again.

Jungle Village Sunset

Dusk is falling. The evening light that puts soft edges on everything filters in from the west and makes even the rough huts look homey and inviting. The setting of the sun gives a break from the heat, and cool breezes begin to flow. Smoke from the cooking fires scents the air. The occasional sound of chickens squabbling over roosting spots is the only break in the silence. The village is quiet and peaceful. This is a jungle village sunset.

I am sitting in the dining room of the bungalow in the village of Itapu. The table and floor are made of hand-hewn hardwood slabs two inches thick and of varying width. Worn smooth by use, they would be worth a fortune if I could get them to America. The walls are woven bamboo that has aged to a light honey color. The ceiling is vaulted; its rafters and supporting structure are made of unfinished logs. The roof is grass that has been twisted and tied onto lengths of bamboo, which are fastened onto the rafters, creating a thick and, in this case, an almost rain-proof thatch.

The walls of the dining room are only four feet high, yielding panoramic views of the surrounding village. Before me is an extinct crater, or as the locals would refer to it, the eye of the volcano. The rim of the crater has been planted with a riotous variety of flowering shrubs and decorative plants. From the floor of the crater, palms and giant tree ferns grow tall. The tops of these trees would normally tower over their surrounding environment, but they reach only eye level from their crater floor base, giving me the fleeting sensation of a bird's eye view. Beyond the crater, the village houses spread out around a nasara, which is dominated by the sacred guardians, huge carvings of local deities or protecting spirits.

I am alone at the table watching the fading light. The rest of our ministry team has walked to a neighboring village, where a chief has invited us all for a meal. I went with them to meet the chief; however, the meal preparations were progressing on "island time" and this was my last evening in the village of Itapu. Tonight I had promised to meet with the new converts for the last teaching and Bible study we would have together, too precious of an occasion to miss. So I wait, knowing that after darkness falls they will be joining me here.

I am straining to absorb all of the ambiance possible. I do not know when, if ever, I will sit here again. My ministry covers a vast area containing thousands of villages. Since I focus on pioneer evangelism and church planting, that frequently means that I spend several weeks in a village helping a local pastor establish a church and then leave, often to never return again, pulled always onward by a never-ending list of villages still needing a gospel witness. Opportunities can't be put off till the next visit. I have learned to seize the moment—climb the mountain, swim in that river, peek over the rim of the volcano, baptize that new convert, play with the children…I may never pass this way again.

In this context, I spend nearly every waking moment trying to make it count. There is little in the way of casual conversation. Words are too precious to be wasted. From morning till night, I am teaching, sometimes in formal classes, but more often in simple dialogue. A never-ending list of questions confront me, and my Bible is worn and tattered from these occasions. Most queries I could answer from memory, quoting relevant passages, but it is vital that they learn the source of truth is not I but the scriptures. So we thumb through the pages together. Is there a greater privilege than to help a first-generation Christian gain a solid footing?

This is ground zero discipleship. My classrooms are many and varied; in this dining room, at the side of the nasara, under the shadow of the guardians, or under a mango, nakatambal, guava, namamba, or towering banyan tree. My students range from gray-bearded old men to timid shy women, eager young children, or an anxious new pastor. The questions deal with foundational issues like the nature of God, sin, and life to seemingly ridiculous inquiries that are often the fruits of the teaching of local cults.

This is my third visit to Itapu. The first was greeted with hostile questions and a begrudging invitation to return. The second was far more receptive and included marking out ground for a church building. This visit was unscheduled but has been the longest so far at nearly a week and has been very productive. I have been able to assist in the construction of the church building and to hold services each evening. I don't know if there will ever be a fourth visit.

The darkness covers the village like a blanket, slowly blotting out the edges of my vision and steadily shrinking the circle of my horizon. I try valiantly to capture images for my memory before the evening erases them. Finally, I am sitting in complete shadow, unable to see even my hands resting on the table before me. I wait. I hear the scrape of sandals on the sandy volcanic ash, the soft clinking of dishes being carried wrapped in a table cloth, and the murmur of conversation between a mother and her children. Their footfalls are approaching the dining room. Supper is coming.

On the far side of the crater, the small, warm light of a kerosene lantern emerges from a hut and slowly bobs and weaves its way up the footpath. As it approaches, the accompanying hand, arm, and attached body become visible until a whole person appears with shining eyes and sparkling white teeth and sets the lantern before me on the table, where it creates a bubble of cheerful light in the midst of the darkness.

Hands appear in the light bearing a plate overburdened with food and a glass of murky water. A soft voice urges me to eat, and the hands retreat to the darkness. As I eat I listen to the sounds around me. More footfalls on the path, feet scuffing the floorboards, and timbers creaking as people settle themselves on the floor, filling up the corners before spreading out along the walls. Slowly the small building fills, and I hear the shuffling of feet of those that cannot find seats and whispered conversations.

I finish my evening meal and stand before the table with my back to the wall. My eyes slowly adjust to the dim light, and the crowd seems to emerge from the shadows. My smile is reflected back in sparkling eyes and glistening teeth. For what may be my last chance with this group of believers, I say, "Let us pray."